Conventionally Speaking

Book One:
For the Love of the Con

Edited by Sally L. Gage and Leisa A. Clark

Copyright © 2019 Sally L. Gage and Leisa A. Clark

All rights reserved. Published by MHP Publishing, St. Petersburg, FL

Photos and Art are from the contributors' personal collections and they retain ownership and copyright. Photos from Lips Down on Dixie (Ward chapter) used with permission from Aron Siegel, C.A.S. / Production Sound Mixer/"Ambitions" S1/ Ambitions Productions. VinyLm@aol.com. FCC LP License WQPV692

No parts of this publication may be reproduced, stored in a retrieval system, or transmitted in any form or by any means, electronic, mechanical, photocopying, recording, or otherwise, without the prior written permission of the copyright owner.

This book is sold subject to the condition that it shall not, by way of trade or otherwise, be lent, resold, hired out, or otherwise circulated without the publisher's prior consent in any form of binding or cover other than that in which it is published and without a similar condition including this condition being imposed on the subsequent purchaser. Under no circumstances may any part of this book be photocopied for resale.

The personal views and opinions expressed in this volume are those of the authors and do not necessarily reflect the official policy or position of any of the Conventions named herein. Any content provided by our contributors/authors are of their opinion, and are not intended to malign any religion, ethic group, club, organization, company, individual, or anyone or anything.

Cover Art by Sally L. Gage

ISBN: 9781093408454

CONVENTIONALLY SPEAKING

DEDICATION

- ❖ To all the Nerds and Wanna Be Nerds
- ❖ To all the Convention-goers near and far, old and young
- ❖ To YOU

TABLE OF CONTENTS

Introduction: For the Love of the Con   3
    Leisa A. Clark

I: THERE'S A FIRST TIME FOR EVERYTHING

1. The Soul of the Con   13
    Kora Addington
2. That First Convention--OMG, Where the Hell Are We and Who is That?   27
    Charlayne Elizabeth Denney
3. Journey to the Center of the Con   41
    Sadie Blackburn
4. Internet Friends are the Best Friends   55
    Joyce McGuire

II. FOR THE LOVE OF THE CON

5. Taking Over the Whole Library   69
    Valerie Estelle Frankel
6. Badges of Honor   81
    Marci Bretts
7. Fun and Games with Con Celebrities   91
    Kathy Lockwood
8. The Unexpected Being of Stella   101
    Sally L. Gage

III. EXCELLENT ECLECTIC ADVENTURES

9. A Very (Mega) Convention Experience   113
    Dee Fish
10. "I'm Just Here for the Backstreet Boys"   125
    Mara Sansolo
11. Star(k) Trek   133
    Brandy Stark
12. WerePups, Conventions, and Emotion   147
    Terry Oakes Paine
13. A *Rocky* Weekend   157
    Thomas Ward

About the Contributors and Editors   169

Book One: For the Love of the Con

ACKNOWLEDGMENTS

We would like to thank all of our contributors and would-be contributors (we will catch some of you next time around—just TRY to back out!). YOUR stories are what make this book—and our future projects—possible. We appreciate your time, effort, and most of all, your willingness to share so many personal tales, experiences, tribulations, and exaltations with us and with the world. We love you all and hope to work with you again!

INTRODUCTION: FOR THE LOVE OF THE CON
Leisa A. Clark

Although the date and place of the first fan convention is under dispute, there is evidence that the premier event was Worldcon, held in the Caravan Hall in New York from July 2 to July 4, 1939[1]. Although there is no record of it, it is certainly possible that fans began officially gathering to share, explore, and celebrate all things nerdy even earlier, since Jules Verne, Mary Shelley, Edgar Allen Poe, Robert Lewis Stevenson, and H.G. Wells were all publishing speculative fiction in the 1800s. And where there is publishing, there is discourse: people love to get together and discuss what they like … and what they dislike … about the fandoms they love.

Fast forward to the 1970s, when many small conventions, such as the New York *Star Trek* Convention (1972) and San Diego Comic-Con (1970), attracted hundreds of fans and a number of celebrities and writers associated with various genres. By the end of 1990s, San Diego Comic-Con had blossomed from ~150 guests to 42,000 to more than double that number by 2005. Similarly, local conventions such as Atlanta's Dragon Con and Orlando's MegaCon Convention have grown significantly and exponentially over the past 20 years.

---

[1] http://fanac.org/worldcon/NYcon/w39-p00.html

So, what happened in the past few decades to turn small-localized groups of fans (gathering to share comic books, toys, memorabilia, and fan-fiction) into worldwide corporate events attracting upwards of 50,000-100,000 guests in one weekend? There are a lot of social, cultural, political, economic, and anthropological explanations for this upswing in fan attendance, but we believe it comes down to one important thing: the fans.

Sally and I have been going to conventions separately and together for more than thirty years. We both started out as wide-eyed  fans who had no idea what to expect from a "fan convention"—especially in the late 1980s and early 1990s, when it was anything but "cool" to sit in a hot hotel conference space just for the chance to maybe have a photo taken with someone who was once on *Star Trek*. But we did it for the love of the convention experience.

It doesn't matter if the convention is in one room at a hotel in downtown St. Petersburg, FL or if it takes up six full hotels in Atlanta, GA: what makes the convention-going experience so amazing, exciting, and—sometimes—terrifying is the sense of fitting in a particular space in time with others who also fit in that place with you. There is an evolutionarily motivated need for a shared sense of belonging to a culture, or in this case a subculture, that allows one a sense of identity. We all have a need to know who we are, who we belong to, and who belongs to us. At fan conventions, this can be expressed through something as simple as just being there to cosplaying an obscure character and grinning with excitement when the source is recognized by someone else. It can be waiting in a long line for a rare collector item, sifting through boxes upon boxes of used comic books looking for a gem, and (pre-YouTube) seeking out the elusive bootlegged copy of the dreadful *Star Wars Holiday Special* from 1978 (on VHS tape no less!). It can be wandering the Vendor

rooms, watching the costume contests, or meeting a celebrity from your childhood (I still plotz that I have not only met, but conversed at length with, Erin Grey from *Buck Rogers in the 25th Century*). It can be any or all of these things…and more.

One evening, Sally and I got into a lengthy conversation about convention memories ("remember that time Gil Gerard called you from across the room to come hang out with him?" or "Remember that time Sean Astin remembered meeting you 20 years earlier?" or "Remember that time John Barrowman sang 'She's Having My Baby' while presenting Katie Cassidy one of the WerePups?"). We were both laughing and enjoying the stories, as we reflected on what conventions mean to us. Over the years, we had grown from wide-eyed young attendees to appearing as Guests and Panel participants.

Attending conventions had truly become part of our identities.

I realized early into the conversation that I wanted to explore what keeps fans returning year after year. Because we both have degrees in Anthropology, Sally and I considered everything from "going back to grad school to get a Ph.D. in Convention Studies" (is there such a thing? There should be!) to "there must be grants out there to support us going to conventions to write a book." But the

more we talked about it, the more we started asking the question: "what do we really want from this project?" For Sally, it was the chance to hear stories. She collects stories and loves nothing more than to sit and listen to others share their experiences. For me, it was a chance to move away from the academically rigorous book editing and teaching I have been doing for the past seven years, and get back to writing things I feel good about. I am not saying academic books don't make me feel good; but they are more about career and less about fun. Conventions have always been about fun for me.

The more we talked about doing this book—and expanding it to a full series—the more enthusiastic we got. It was the most exciting thing we had chosen to work on in a long time and we were eager to get started. But the question we still needed to focus on was "how."

Did we want to try to get grants, travel around to conventions, and interview fans? Would that even be possible? Did we actually have the time, money, and energy for such an endeavor? And, the bottom line really was that we wanted to hear the stories of others told in their own voices. So, we decided to go with the age-old academic collection model: but to do it our way. We wrote up a proposal and shared it in various Facebook groups, focusing on those that were devoted to various conventions. We asked friends and family as well. After a couple of months, we had more proposals than could possibly fit into one book. The idea of a series of books germinated over too much coffee and the difficulties in choosing which stories we wanted for this book.

In the end, I am excited with the essays we chose, and with the people who volunteered their time and stories towards making this

book possible. Ultimately it is THEIR stories that we hope you will enjoy reading as much as we did. Some are funny and some are poignant. All are moving in their own ways. Many talk about how they felt attending conventions for the first time or what it is like to be a guest under varying circumstances. Quite a few of the book's contributors discuss their "celebrity encounters"—so much so that we realized we can do an entire book just on that exciting aspect of the con-going experience!

Before I forget, I want to make a note about the celebrities mentioned in this book. Most of our contributors encountered different celebrities at conventions, and of course, they wanted to write about them and share those experiences with readers. Not all of the descriptions are flattering, but they are real. When names are named, it is because the author felt that it was necessary for context. All of the contributors who discuss celebrities acknowledge that it is *their personal experience* with the individuals in question and that these may not be the same experiences others have had. Look, celebrities are people too—and as such, they have good and bad days, just like we do. Some are notoriously grumpy with fans (and this is no secret), while others are always kind and gracious, even when sick or exhausted. Each of us has met celebrities we did not enjoy meeting—and then heard from others who had wonderful meetings with the same person—sometimes at the same convention! Essays about personal experiences are exactly that: conversations about *personal* experiences of individual fans with individual celebrities. You may not agree—that may not have been *your* experience—and that is okay. Under no circumstances is anyone trying to malign or denigrate anyone by sharing their stories here.

There are so many stories here—and these are just the tip of a vast fandom iceberg. In Part One: There's a First Time for Everything, long-time Con attendees discuss their first time...at conventions, that is. Kora Addington reflects on being an outsider looking in…and how wonderful it was to attend her first convention, while Charlayne Elizabeth Denney remembers the eye-opening shock of working as a Vendor at a Convention in the 1970s. Sadie Blackburn remains a reluctant con-goer, but she muses about her experiences being an invited guest author who had never even been to a convention. Finally, Joyce McGuire's first con experience was at the mother of all cons: San Diego Comic-Con!

In Part Two: For the Love of the Con, we explore different sides of the convention-going experience. Valerie Estelle Frankel looks at the smaller, local Library-based conventions that have become popular in the past few years, while Marci Bretts explores the ways that being a Badge-holder at a convention is a ticket into a whole new world. Kathy Lockwood and Sally Gage both talk about their own fan experiences meeting new people, engaging with celebrities, and exploring conventions over the years.

In Part Three: Excellent Eclectic Adventures, Dee Fish shares her experiences as a trans woman navigating the often-difficult concerns of being an LGBTQ+ guest at a convention in conservative States. Mara Sansolo has a completely different experience from others who shared stories in this volume, in that she is not really a convention fan at all; but where the Backstreet Boys go, she follows, even to Horror Conventions! Conversely, Brandy Stark and Terry Oakes Paine are both frequent attendees who have had their own share of exciting and interesting fan encounters over the years, while attending with family and friends. Last but not least, Thomas Ward imparts his humorous take on performing in a shadow cast of *The*

Rocky Horror Picture Show…at Dragon Con no less!

Fandom and fan conventions are a major part of our lives and the increased attendance at so many events proves that they are not going anywhere. Whether you are a longtime convention-goer or if you are not sure what to expect at one, we hope you will enjoy the stories in this book as they are intended: to celebrate the Love of the Con.

PART ONE

There's a First Time for Everything

Book One: For the Love of the Con

1 THE SOUL OF THE CON
Kora Addington

On the 14th floor of the Hyatt Atlanta, I stare at my reflection in the bathroom mirror. The warm white vanity lights make my eyes—no longer behind the lenses of my glasses—pop ethereally, my pupils huge, taking everything in. My heart sinks a little. I can't help but feel how I always have about finally being here, at Dragon Con in Atlanta.

It's the feeling of never believing you'll get into your dream college; or leaving the interview after an application for a great job feeling sick to your stomach that you didn't sell yourself well enough; or leaving a party with the overshadowing gremlin of a thought that everyone is glad you're gone.

Imposter syndrome, anxiety, heartache; there are many ways to say it. Whatever it was, I had always felt it about Dragon Con.

I look myself over. My hand-sewn tunic with embroidered golden Hylian crest emblazoned across the chest and my skirt with *Ocarina of Time*-style music notes dancing across plain white folds of fabric over pink and purple tulle feel stiff and cold on my body.

When I was a teenager, I used to watch the other kids get ready to come to Atlanta—right in our Georgian backyard—for the con every year. I used to hate them: the Dungeons and Dragons *boys (I have since learned to my personal happiness that the game, like so many other things worth participating in and enjoying, is neither as segregated nor as gendered as I was once led to believe), the kids who grew up in "nerd" families, or intact families in general, and the crowd that made it a tradition to go every year. For the out-of-sync, out-of-community, and out-of-money, going to conventions for such a thing as genuine fun was never within reach before, and thus, never even within dreaming.*

For my costume, I've taken an old athletic shirt to wear underneath the tunic and I've added my own handmade gold aluminum chain-maille cuffs for a *Twilight Princess* look. It took me about a month total that summer to make my purple version of the Master Sword and sheath, its constituent parts a child's foam ninja sword, ninety-nine-cent foam sheets from the craft store, paper towel rolls, copious amounts of hot glue, and lots of paint and sealant.

I grew up in a Chronicles of Narnia-*fanatic,* Lord of the Rings-*adoring, magic and believing and mythology-loving family. As a Middle Schooler I spent hours every night writing my own historical fantasy fiction, researching constructed fantasy languages and creatures. There should have been nothing I did not love about the world of cosplay and conventions, and yet, I hated it when people recalled their con experiences. I saw them, and I saw everything I felt I couldn't be, with the limitations of my single-parent family, financial struggle, and worst of all, self-doubt fed by the sense that in high school I joined a community whose members had known each other all their lives. I resented their cosplays, and even the word "cosplay." I would try to block them out when they detailed their months of planning, which would always lead up to Labor Day weekend, and their laughing and smiling over shared moments, conversations, and interactions with others at the con. I hated it all because, in the end, it was never shared with me.*

CONVENTIONALLY SPEAKING

*My family bought games and did nerdy things together sometimes. In the 3rd grade I played—and certainly did not finish—*The Legend of Zelda II: Link's Adventure *on my very first game system, the Gameboy Advance SP, and later on, when I was in late Middle School, our family played* Twilight Princess *(which I feel like was really my first dive into* Legend of Zelda *fandom),* Skyward Sword, *and lots of cheap trade-in games from GameStop. But outside the walls of my home, hardly anyone else recognized my desire to share in that interest and participation elsewhere. In an attempt to make me feel better about saying "No" to that desire, my High School boyfriend had told me, "Eh you wouldn't be that into it" when I asked if I could sit in on his* Dungeons and Dragons *campaign with his friends. I learned the main reason he told me that was to keep the numbers low, even though only a few months later they let in another girl, and after that, a landslide of new people joined in. He also at one point told me he wasn't interested in even trying to read any of my fiction work, because it wasn't his "cup of tea." So, I didn't try, because rejections like that made me feel as if no one would want me to. I didn't try to play* Dungeons and Dragons.

I felt the "in" crowd thought I was too slow, with my observe-first-play-later style of learning, given the fact that I didn't grow up with a personal computer or access to these exciting things before and hadn't had experience, like others did, interacting with games that were now in their third or fourth or fifth generation since first being developed. Even though I could sight-translate Latin and write speeches and spoof Doctor Horrible *newspaper articles for our school, the assumption seemed to be that* Magic the Gathering *and* StarCraft *and roleplaying stats were too complicated for me; that it just wasn't a good match, that I should just go away and try something else. So, I went away to go knit and drink blueberry tea, and watch weird documentaries with my collection of mostly female friends, which I enjoyed and still love—but it felt to be more automatically and solely my place over our local gaming and nerd community. I didn't go watch the Dragon Con parade or ask my con-going friends, with their big con-going families and bigger con-going buddy circles, about how the convention went every year, because it hurt too much to. Nobody asked me if I wanted to Pokémon battle or go to the* Legend of Zelda *symphony—which I very much wanted to go to but was told it was a boys' trip and I wouldn't have much fun. I avoided seeing my friends' pictures on social media when they got together without me at the con, because they did, and they looked happy, too. I tried to act like I wasn't interested. I bought into the denial, because it was at least a way to deal with the exclusion.*

The last thing I do, after checking my boots, pulling on warm fingerless gloves with the Triforce of Wisdom woven onto the back of one hand, and fiddling with my trick-shop elf ears and the accompanying prosthetic tacky, is to place the iconic cap on my head and barrette it into place. Rather than being green, it matches my color scheme—a white foundation, with lines of light purple and a gold band on the edge. I look at myself in the mirror one last time and allow myself to smile. I used to hate the very mention of the word; but here I was, wearing my first cosplay ever.

The journey from trying not to cry at the barest mention of Dragon Con in a conversation to showing up wearing my Legend of Zelda *series mashup happened more rapidly than I ever expected. The very act of buying myself my first four-day ticket for 2015 was to treat myself to some self-love, but it had such a sweet tinge of revenge after the D&D boy I'd dated for two years in High School* had ended our emotionally tenuous relationship following the inaugural month of my freshman year at college—he left me over the phone, two days before my first birthday away from home. To a 19-year-old, it was pretty world-shattering. I'd get back at him, back at them all, by showing up to the con the next year and treating myself to something I'd always wanted but never got to have. I made the arrangements to stay with my best friend's family in a host hotel and I tried to decide what I'd wear. "Happy Birthday to me," I thought, whenever I imagined the upcoming Labor Day weekend and my first con and cosplay experience.

That spring, things brightened. I started talking to a guy in my history class who liked to write fantasy science fiction and play games, and whenever I told him about my writing or interests, his world stopped, and he would simply listen. He would immediately offer to let me borrow his game systems or come over to play something I'd never played before. He said he wanted to read my fantasy work. I ended up being his cup of tea, to poetically borrow previous phrasing. The exciting and inspiring reason I decided to design my cosplay after the outfit style of Link and the strength and color palette of Zelda that Dragon Con was because I ended up playing Ocarina of Time 3D that summer when he let me borrow his DS, not even thinking twice about sharing it with me.

We've been together for four years now. At every opportunity he shares this participative universe with me, from the first time I tentatively sat at the keyboard to play—and embarrassingly but hilariously flail around in—a Minecraft-like horror game, to the present day as we play Super Smash Brothers Ultimate. I attempt The Adventure of Link once again, and he discovers his newfound love of restoring and modifying old Gameboy systems. When I played Ocarina of Time that summer of 2015, I experienced a fresh awakening of empowerment and inclusion. All it took was someone willing to give me a step up into this

Book One: For the Love of the Con

world, and I felt the immersion I'd always dreamed of. I feel it again whenever I get to play something new.

That immersion feels shaky as I come out of the bathroom and show off my costume. My best friend, her brother, and their dad, who hosts people every year at the con hotel, smile and give me their thumbs-up of approval. Then they get back to prepping their plans for the day. My boyfriend, who has come just for the day to see the con for the first time himself, makes me smile for a picture, but I just don't feel *right* about it yet.

We walk out of the hotel room together and we run into the old *D&D* boy group from high school right outside the door in the hallway. They ask me what I'm *supposed* to be. It's not malicious, as they seemed to be trying to piece the look together, but at the same time, it's not seeking genuine attention or kindness.

"I'm a Zelda/Link mashup," I say, trying to grin. The kid I  used to date looks at me and my current companion as the color drains from his face. The girl he left me for answers my explanation with an "Oh, cool." She looks anywhere but my eyes. She spots the details of the skirt, the *Song of Storms* and *Zelda's Lullaby* dancing across the fabric in rushed embroidery, and does point them out, but then awkwardly ends the commentary by explaining how she thought I might have been something else. She's trying her hardest to regain the knowledge in the conversation, but it's suddenly proving difficult. I realize, as we find the earliest convenient moment to walk away and they murmur together behind us, that they are the ones who feel closed off now, as if they feel excluded from this experience I am beginning to own. My gratitude and thankfulness that I was able to come to the con this year bubbles up inside, a satisfaction that now the people who used to tell me this experience wasn't for me are wrong, and now they get to watch me prove it. Of course, that still doesn't show on my face. I still outwardly feel timid and embarrassed, as if I'm hiding behind my cosplay. As we descend into the convention scene, and I take my boyfriend's hand, my new and self-made experience becomes less about the revenge and the snatching back of my teenage feelings of resentment and exclusion, and becomes something much bigger and even more important.

Once out on the open floor of the Hyatt, we can't help but stop and stare. Someone in a full-size fuzzy Pikachu costume, ears poking up out of the crowd, weaves in and out of the traffic, hands held out playfully as he waddles back and forth. A group of mechanized Power Rangers stands for a picture in front of the bluish-purple Dragon Con backdrop close to the elevators. A cluster of Ricks with varying shades of blue, grey, and white hair—because, true to his chaotic nature, it seems no one can collectively decide how his cartoon hair translates to real life—walks by with a few straggling Mortys. The first time I'm brave enough to ask someone for a picture of their costume, it's a *Magic the Gathering* cosplayer, who has created a suit of armor out of playing cards from the game. I've spent so much time just watching people play *Magic* matches (even without facing anyone myself) that I recognize a lot of the cards. She poses in a fighting stance and smiles. I think it's just as exciting and nerve-wracking for her to get asked for a picture as it is for me to ask. I take the photo, trying to take it fast enough to not be in the way of people flooding into the room from the skybridge where a river of con friends flows between host hotels, but not so fast that my slow, cheap phone makes the image blurry. I manage to take an alright shot and thank her for waiting, both of us smiling wide.

My boyfriend and I explore the hotel floor by floor, marveling at the art shows and the costume contests. I try to remember all the  drawings I want to come back and buy if I can, with the little leftover money I still have after all the work that went into my cosplay. We watch the boisterous groups of revelers outwardly exclaiming what we feel—an overwhelming enjoyment and celebration of liking things: Games, movies, shows, anime, manga, cartoons, books, lore, it doesn't matter. There is a spiritual kind of magic in the air, and it's made up of people's love for these worlds, and as an extension, their own world for providing them with these things they love.

As we get to the very bottom floor and the crowds thin, my boyfriend asks to snap another picture of me and my outfit. He'd been asking lots of strangers for photos, absolutely freaking out at the recognition he feels seeing so many cosplays, and he wants to add me into the mix. "Smile, bb," he says. In that moment, with strangers looking on as I stand for my photo, my exuberance overtakes me. I smile. Now, it feels so real.

The popularity and prevalence of cosplay arrives at such a good time, not just for me, but for everyone looking for a place to belong. The world is full of talk about well-being: mental health awareness, self-care and the fading stigma that surrounds it, body positivity, and intersectional movements for equality across the board. Cosplay enters the conversation unexpectedly, and yet so fittingly. Cosplay says, "It doesn't matter who you are, or what you look like; if you love something, you're free to be a part of it." Conventions are home to crossplay, genderbending, homebrewing, people-watching, and most of all, simply creating. Showing up is its own kind of inclusion. "I think cosplay is just a natural outlet for the innate human desire to be socially engaged and recognized for something. It just happens to also be combined with something creative and awesome," writes Kyle Johnsen, one of many cosplayers, crafters, and social media promoters featured in the convention and cosplay experience book collection Cosplay World *(43)*[2].

It's not just the enjoyment of your own cosplay experience that is exciting and sustaining, between the brain-storming, planning, making, and finally, wearing; there's so much more enjoyment on top of all that which comes from experiencing cosplay through seeing it in others. When you recognize and appreciate the work and homage to something well-loved, big or small, that someone has built, and they are able to receive it, there's a great connection and interaction with something bigger than any individual.

---

[2] Ashcraft, Brian, and Luke Plunkett. Cosplay World. Prestel Verlag, 2014.

Book One: For the Love of the Con

That first year, I proudly wore my Zelda/Link costume all Saturday...which also happened to be my 20th birthday. My year had turned full-circle, from feeling alone and excluded, both relationally and socially, to being included and surrounded by people who valued what I'd always loved: art, characters, games, stories, and the love of liking what other people create. Being allowed, rather than barred from, participation is magical. People approached me to complement the pieces of my outfit, or sometimes, because of the nature of crowds, were made to notice them (such as the sword on my back which sometimes got in the way) but said very kind things anyway.

At our second Dragon Con, my boyfriend and I designed urban versions of the outfits of the Travelers from the PlayStation 3 game *Journey*, turning flowing robes and sashes into hoodies and backpacks. Over the course of the next year, I was finally able to really play a full campaign of *Dungeons and Dragons* for myself, so the following con, I came as my elf druid character, and even though I didn't have the time or money then, in my senior year of college, to put together the kind of outfit I wanted, I was able to craft a lovely druid staff, complete with branched tendrils, greenery, and flowers. I still love keeping it on the wall in my room, along with my Princess Zelda-fied Master Sword and *Journey* mask. Every year as I put together and wore another cosplay, I felt more and more myself, by creating and embodying ideas and imagining experiences that are nothing like my real life; or, maybe, they encompass more of what life means than I ever thought. I've heard something speak to me often over the years of con participation, in the moments I am alone, and in those moments when both friends and strangers make brief but joyous contact with me over the shared love of things, which I can liken to nothing else except a kind of soul: The Soul of the Con.

Paulo Coelho's The Alchemist, *a lovely and rich story about a shepherd boy searching for his treasure and living out his "Personal Legend," mentions an integral presence to living and dreaming throughout its narrative, which it calls "the Soul of the World." It is something alive and beneficent, a "language without words," connecting people and feelings with fates and personal legends: "When you want something with all your heart, that's when you are closest to the Soul of the World. It's always a positive force" (Coelho 81)[2]. The Soul of the Con is a lot like this. It is an-ever present spirit in every hallway, lobby, street corner, conference room, and sleeping space at the host hotels. It's in the flashes of color at late-night raves, the music and laughter on the skybridges, and even the stillness of the Atlanta night when you pop your head outside to take a relatively cool, clear breath of air. It is something we can talk to, which listens and presents us with the things which delight us, which connects us to living and enjoying the things we like to love, even when we're not surrounded by wholeheartedly content fans feeling at home in the environment the con provides. It even connects us to those we have enjoyed the con with, but whom we have lost since. They are still with us. It gifts us with all the beautiful moments we take home when we leave, and it is what*

---

[2] Coelho, Paulo. The Alchemist, 25th Anniversary Edition. HarperOne, 2014.

beckons us to return again and again. The wonderful part is that the Soul of the Con also changes with us year to year. It is always seeking to connect us to the world around us, at whatever level of fandom we might inhabit.

I'm three years removed from that moment in time, on the bottom floor of the Hyatt, grinning shyly but ecstatically; when I connected to the Soul of the Con and knew that everything that had seemed off-limits for me before and the world from which I'd felt excluded had become mine to own and experience, too. Since then, I've returned to Atlanta every Labor Day weekend to experience what had never seemed to be *for me*. Every year, I've claimed a little more of what makes the con so vibrant, so exciting, and so hard to leave. The first year, we tried to see everything there was to see, which of course was impossible. The next year, we went to lots of panels and seminars. The year after that, we probably spent half the weekend waiting in line to see short film collections and panels with the occasional con celebrity. This past year, we stayed out late every night with our friends, playing *Pokémon Go*, randomly stumbling into different gatherings and spots of interest, and watching Studio Ghibli movies. During the day we'd play board games, nap, and find tiny corners in the food court to eat. All of these different experiences were pieces of fandom paradise, and yet, no two years have really been alike.

Bizarrely, my favorite year so far has been this past year, when I took a break from cosplaying altogether. It's not that the lack of cosplaying made it better—and I honestly missed cosplaying—but I couldn't dress up because I had just started my first post-college job. I was broke, and my best friend generously ended up buying my and my boyfriend's tickets as a gift right before the con. The Soul of the Con opened up its arms and invited us in anyway. This year's Dragon Con felt like a temporary foray into an alternate world, a world where you could simply be; everyone feels in high spirits, alive, seeking out what makes them feel giddy with nerdy glee. It was during this con, as our friend group spent so much time together bonding and relaxing, that I could take a step back and realize how much I'd enjoyed cosplaying in years past, in going from fandom exclusion to inclusion. At this con, I was able to look down on the problems and heartaches of the past year, as if looking down on earth from *Serenity* or the Starship *Enterprise* and realize that I wasn't as stuck or as hopeless because of things that had happened to me in my last year of college as I had thought. I've still struggled with these difficulties since, but with renewed passion, enjoyment, and a sense of ultimate belonging, my life seems to be charting a new trajectory, and I'm so excited now, after the revelations of Dragon Con 2018, to see where it all goes.

Over the last year, I've found great comfort and euphoric enjoyment settling into hours (well over 200, more hours than the game can completely track in Hero's Path Mode) of playing Breath of the Wild, *solely because I love it. I ask for games for my birthday and Christmas now. At my job, I ran a* Dungeons and Dragons *session for a dozen middle schoolers as a first-time Dungeon Master, and even after leaving that position, they still ask the department for more and more game time. I relax with some* eeveelution *coloring sheets with my colleagues, who have complemented me on my Dragon Con lanyard, which I use for work (I use another from the con last year for my keys.) I'm surrounded by fandom and shared liking of things, by people of all ages. At the present moment, I'm working two jobs and taking on double shifts to pay for my future cosplays, games, and other adventures, including marrying the person who held out a hand for me to join in this shared wonderful feeling of inclusiveness in fandom, and who, along with the friends I've kept and made since those first college days, gave me the encouragement and support to be connected to the Soul of the Con. I'm doing whatever it takes so I can buy my four-day ticket for Dragon Con 2019. Going to the con, immersing myself in loving things, and ultimately, loving myself, are all too important to not work hard for. Even as I count down the months and days to the con this year, I claim more and more of that participation and fandom acceptance found out in the world, sensing the guidance of the Soul of the Con until we come once again face to face.*

2 THAT FIRST CONVENTION—OMG, WHERE THE HELL ARE WE AND WHO IS THAT?
Charlayne Elizabeth Denney

1979. My first year hanging out in fandom.

Growing up in Amarillo Texas (read: blessed middle of nowhere), there was very little ability to join in fandom activities. I had never heard of science fiction/*Star Trek* conventions until I met my two best friends (now my siblings of heart), Lynn and Arthur, who introduced me to that world. Arthur took me to my first convention, SuperCon, in Houston over Thanksgiving.

This was a huge deal for a 22-year-old from the Texas panhandle. Up until then, I hadn't been out of the city much except with my parents. This was all the way to Houston. A long 600 miles away, 11 hours. Arthur was selling knives, swords, and replica weapons and he had booked us a table at the Whitehall in downtown Houston. We drove down with the back of the pickup loaded with all sorts of shiny, pointy, bang-toys. The time went pretty fast on the trip, right until we got to Houston.

Have I mentioned that Houston is huge? Or that the roads don't make sense? Or that there's an elevated highway going around downtown, and the hotel sits on one side of the highway? Yeah, going into downtown, the roads look like a spaghetti bowl exploded and roads go everywhere, except to the hotel.

We got lost. We kept circling the downtown area but never could get there from here, wherever "here" was. At one point, I made Arthur stop and let me buy a city map. I was hoping the roads would make more sense if I could see them on the map. I started trying to guide us in, "Turn right, turn left, now right again, OOPS!"

We got into a rather seedy part of town just outside what I later learned was the Pierce Elevated. And we could *see* the hotel but there was no signage to get to downtown. I honestly think Arthur ran at least two stop signs and crossed someone's lawn trying to get to the one road that we thought would get us there. Luckily, we chose the right string of spaghetti and got to the hotel, got checked in, unloaded the truck, and started to set up.

This was on Thanksgiving Thursday, the night before the event was to open at 10 a.m. Friday. The schedule included a reception with a buffet for the dealers who came in early and the guests of the  convention. As I heaped fresh shrimp onto my plate, I asked Art where the stars were. He gestured to a very tall man talking quietly to a group of convention staff. "That is the body of Darth Vader, David Prowse." I had known Darth was more than one person, between voice and body (and later a face) but at 6 feet 6 inches, Prowse stood well over the other people in the room.

Art then pointed at a couple of guys talking with another group. They were the physical effects team from *Texas Chainsaw Massacre*. The first one, which had come out in 1974, the year before I graduated high school. The one that had scared me; I was still having periodic nightmares starring a guy with a chainsaw.

Art continued his narration: "Scotty from *Star Trek*—Jimmy Doohan—will be here tomorrow sometime, he's finishing his part of the audio dubbing for *Star Trek the Motion Picture (STTMP)*." He was one person I was hoping to see.

"See that big bunch of girls over there? Inside that knot is Anthony Daniels…C3PO," Art pointed out.

I instantly was intrigued. "Go get his autograph for me!" I begged.

"No, you go get it yourself."

"But…he's a big star, I can't talk to him." Yes, I was that terrified. I'd never previously met anyone who had been in a movie. Much less one that was so defining of nerd-culture in the late 1970s.

Art simply took my plate of shrimp out of my hands, laid it on the table nearby, and walked me across the room. The group of women parted like the Red Sea in *The Ten Commandments* and Art pushed me right up in front of a very nicely dressed man.

"Mr. Daniels, this is Charlie. You're her first big star; talk to her."

That rat Art walked away, leaving me standing there stammering with my mouth wide open!

But I have to say, Anthony Daniels is one of the nicest guys I ever met in fandom. He not only talked to me, I was invited to dinner and the VIP NASA tour with him.

By the next day, as dawn broke over downtown Houston, rumors were swirling about the possibility that Leonard Nimoy would be stopping by and doing an appearance at the convention. I called back to Amarillo to tell Lynn, who grabbed a few things, jammed them into a suitcase, and flew down for the convention. We also found out that the ABC television show *20/20* was going to be there filming for their segment on the opening of the *STTMP* movie, scheduled to premiere in a couple of weeks.

Friday of the convention was pretty much typical convention. We got to our table shortly before 10 a.m. and got everything arranged for sale. Art was worried that the door between the dealer's room and one of the big panel rooms wasn't locked and our standing display of weapons was in front of it. We were assured by the convention committee's dealer coordinator that the door would be locked and guarded so there would be no mishaps.

Even with assurances, the door was opened at least four times during the day, spilling weaponry all over the booth. The last time, I had just stepped from behind the table when the display fell again. This time a revolver had the sight broken off. Arthur grabbed it and madly hurdled himself out of the room in search of the con-chairman who had previously (or originally) authorized the assurances that this wouldn't happen. I learned later that the convention ended up buying a replica revolver that day.

As with many conventions, hall costumes, those wonderful incarnations of superheroes, ships captains, and aliens of all colors and kinds, were seen all over the hotel, especially on Saturday, when the costume contest was scheduled. Cosplay, as it's now called, wasn't called that back in the 1970s; then, it was just "costumes" and people would try to get them to look like they did in the movies and television shows. This was back well before we had good photos to work from (much less access to the internet where you can see the entire costume, blow up the picture to get the details) and before the moldable foam that is available now.

Back then, would-be costumers had to find a copy of *Starlog* Magazine, or a *TV Guide* with photos and then use a magnifying glass to try to get the details. And some costumes were made from the weirdest items. *Star Trek: The Motion Picture* had some very strange uniforms: the bottoms honestly looked like boots under footie pajamas. So, ours had footy pajamas and we wore tennis shoes under them. I know I wore out at least three sets of bottom material wearing mine. I also had the belt that was worn in *STTMP* and if you look very closely, it looks somewhat like a rectangular reflector for a bicycle. We took it, did some paint work and glued it to the material we used for a belt. You had to use whatever you had on hand to get some of these costumes. Unfortunately, at the time of the convention, there had been no photos leaked of those uniforms, so we had to think of something else to do since copying them was not an option yet.

Still, in spite of the limitations, the costumes of that era were very good, carefully constructed down to the littlest detail possible. The ones at the convention were very eye-opening, so many different ones, some better than others. From original *Star Trek* costumes, newer designs of the new space opera: *Battlestar Galactica*, superheroes of all universes, to the various aliens and denizens of *Star Wars* and the Mos Eisley bar scene were all there in the main halls of the convention.

When we started trying to figure out costumes for the night, Art did his 1920s gangster outfit (a nod to the original *Star Trek* episode "A Piece of the Action." Lynn's was the problem; she hadn't had anything in mind when she just threw random things into her suitcase. She had brought with her a long piece of yellow lace, a necklace, and, for some weird reason, a box of assorted food coloring. We came up with a black skirt and a black bandeau top, but the food coloring had us stumped. Then we hit on it: the Andorians, from the original series, were blue. So, we took the blue food coloring and mixed it with the very light Cover Girl makeup I had.

But we hadn't thought this through. Even though the makeup was light, it still had a good bit of yellow pigment in it. Blue and yellow make...green.

We panicked at first, trying to figure out how we would explain this one. It certainly wasn't Andorian blue. Then Lynn remembered the Orion slave girls in the original series were green. So, she became an Orion as I smeared that green makeup all over her feet, midline, her arms, legs, and back. She got her face and I put the mixture on the back of her neck. A bit of baby powder to set it, and the gold necklace gently laid into her black hair, hanging down on her forehead, completed the look. I slipped on the coveralls and pilot's helmet Art had brought for me and he wore part of another uniform.

As we left the hotel room, we looked back at the bathroom. It looked like we had slaughtered a good-sized Vulcan in that room. Green stuff was all over the place. Once the costume contest was over, we made a valiant attempt to clean it up but there was still a green bathtub ring that we didn't manage to get out. Before we checked out, we left a bit of money for the housekeeper; the poor woman was going to have a battle with that ring.

Going downstairs, we came out of the elevator to the second-floor lobby and I saw the most interesting sight. Despite the previous discussion of costumes, and the few I had seen prior to this Saturday night spectacle, I wasn't prepared for the amount of people dressed up. There were Supermen, a variety of spacemen (and women), and so many others. We were directed to stand in a line for the contest and somehow Lynn and I got separated. It may have been me standing there staring at everyone's costumes, but I lost track of her. To my surprise, she later told me she had been pulled out of line for the *20/20* crew to interview her. Later, when the show aired, my best friend and sister of the heart got her big shot on national television: dressed in green makeup and lace, saying "I always wanted to be an astronaut." I really wish I had a video of this, but video tape recorders were over $900 each and tapes were over $20 dollars in 1970s money—far above the average fan's reach.

But while she was off doing the interview, I was dutifully standing in line, near the end. I had someone behind me, a guy dressed in a cape, wearing very tall boots with rhinestones lining the sides along the bottom and heel. When I got up to his face, his hair was teased out to a large, curly mess, and he was…wearing makeup??

Remember, I am a kid from the panhandle of Amarillo and it was pretty conservative back in the 1970's and 80s. So, this wasn't just a surprise, it was a shock. But it was not the biggest shock. After picking my jaw up off the floor, I asked him, "What, or who, are you supposed to be?"

"Frankenfurter" came the reply, said with a bit of snark that I obviously had no idea what I was looking at.

So, I obliged him, "What's a Frankenfurter?"

Instead of just explaining that the costume was a character from *The Rocky Horror Picture Show* (which I had never heard of at that time), he opened the cape and I got the full effect: corset, G-string shorts, and fishnet hose in all its glory!

Cue the bigger shock. You could have knocked me over by blowing on me. I just stood there and gaped.

He closed the cape and we talked for a few moments, then it was time for us to go into the panel room with everyone watching. I got up there on the dais, stumbled through a few words "Reporting for duty, ma'am, I mean sir, uh…." My brain just stopped.

There in the middle aisle, to the side, was the camera for *20/20*. They were filming all of this.

All of it. Which became apparent when the next costumed entry started approaching the dais. There was music playing (not all of us had it) and the guy who had been standing behind me—in that cape and makeup—strutted up to the front, hips swaying. He got to the top of the dais (the music changed just a bit) and tapped his right heel three times, then dropped the cape and started strutting around to the song I found out later was "Sweet Transvestite" from *Rocky Horror*.

To say the place went batshit is still an understatement. People were hooting, cheering, whistling, cat-calling, and just exuberantly greeting this "Frankenfurter."

Then, over the din, I could hear someone yelling "Cut! Cut! Cut!" The director was standing in the aisle behind the cameraman, who was obviously ignoring him and just letting the camera roll.

Pandemonium. Simple pandemonium rained in that room for a good five minutes. Then it settled down again. I have no idea who won, it wasn't that important. The magic of all the costumes, and the exuberance of the audience is what I remember of that...and one Sweet Transvestite.

We stumbled back to the hotel room after the costume contest had ended. Walking into the room, we were still trying to process what we had just been involved with. It took us awhile to change clothes, attempt to further clean up the bathroom, and talk about what we saw. All of us were just amazed at the wonder of the entire evening.

Afterward, I had time to see what else SuperCon had to offer. The filking (science fiction/fantasy songs set to folk songs) went on  for hours in one of the panel rooms, another showed movies. These movies were not yet available on DVD or even VHS tape to the average fan yet; as mentioned above, the cost was very high. The film room was showing the films from the theaters; multiple reels that were shown on a small screen in a panel room.

Soon, the convention was over. Lynn packed up and caught the return flight home since she had to work that night. Art and I packed up the dealer's room stock and our suitcases, loading the truck with everything but the stuff from the room that was on the bell cart. One last weapon couldn't be packed, because we had sold something and used the box it came in. That replica Thompson sub-machine gun was hung on the cart as I paid for the hotel room. Art was down starting the truck, because the valet driver couldn't figure it out since it was a cantankerous and temperamental farm pickup that took finesse to start. The cart was momentarily unattended.

As I turned to go back, I noticed that one of the bell boys was playing with my Thompson. Walking up, I took it from him, popped it up to check the sight on it (those broke easily on some models) and promptly got tapped rather hard on the shoulder.

I dropped the gun down to my side as I turned to see a badge in a wallet staring at me. Behind it was a guy dressed in a suit with the earphone coming from his back.

"I'm Captain…so'n'so (I don't remember the name, for reasons that will become apparent) from the Houston Police Department in charge of dignitary protection. Put that damned thing away."

I never heard his name. I was wondering if I was going to get arrested for having a gun without a permit (long before Texas allowed open or even concealed carry). I launched into the sale speech I used, "It's a replica weapon. These are used in place of real ones in movies, it's made out of a special alloy and no firing pin. It will explode if it gets used…."

"I know what that is, what you are doing, who you are, and who your friend is. We ran background checks on you when you arrived. We've been preparing the hotel for a state visit as the convention was packing up. But the Mossad tends to shoot first and ask questions later." The cop pointed up to a building nearby. I could see someone on the roof. Looking back at him, I wrapped my leather jacket around the gun and shoved it under three suitcases.

"Thompson? What Thompson?"

Moshe Dayan, a just retired-minister of defense for Israel was in town to visit a friend and other things and happened to have been in the hotel about 15 minutes as we were vacating.

Thankfully Arthur rescued me about that time by pulling up in the truck. We loaded the last of the stuff and drove through some dreary weather back to the Texas panhandle.

So, this was my first convention. I have many more stories. There would be many, many more cons over the years and I'm still doing them, but now as an author guest.

I've only paid to go to one convention since 1979. I have worked them in every capacity from convention committee, publicity, volunteer, registration desk, guest escort, and panelist. Volunteering to work a convention is the best way to do one, in my opinion. You can get closer to the guests, you can meet all sorts of great folks, and if you do several hours of volunteering over the weekend, you can get into the convention free.

Conventions have changed somewhat since that big Supercon in Houston. Some are smaller, fan-run conventions, others are what we call "pro-cons" done by businesses set up for that, with corporate sponsors. These are the ones you see with guest lists that have several big-named stars on them. They have volunteers as well, but the ability to hob-knob with the guests is limited.

It's been almost 40 years since Supercon, but I still remember it very well and I cherish those memories now. Even with all the other "no shit there I was" stories I have, this one is probably one of the wildest. C2PO, crazy costumes, and that Frankenfurter guy. What memories!

Book One: For the Love of the Con

3 JOURNEY TO THE CENTER OF THE CON: THROUGH THE CONVENTION LOOKING GLASS
Sadie Blackburn

Despite the fact that I (long time Bay Area Renaissance Festival actress, Steampunk writer, and certified admirer of Neil Gaiman and Joss Whedon) likely have more than enough points in my favor to provide me with geek cred, I nevertheless discovered in 2018 that I had managed to live half a century on this planet without ever attending a con. This is not the fault of my friends—authors, graphic novel illustrators, D&D aficionados, virtuoso cosplayers, and werewolf urban legend experts—who have spent the past several years inviting me. The truth is, my attendance at MegaCon (in Tampa, Florida) came about entirely by accident.

Concurrent with the release of my newest book, I participated in a small, local event held at Emerald City Comics in Clearwater, Florida. Enthusiastic and excited, the organizer (who owned a book store) told the gathered company that she planned to go to MegaCon as an exhibitor, and that she thought it would be great for some local authors to attend. To be polite, I smiled and made encouraging noises, only to find myself suddenly scheduled to be a part of an author panel in September. It is ridiculous to report how surprised I was to hear this, but there you have it.

In the weeks leading up to the event, my spurious (if creative) dog and pony show of excuses proved essentially futile, so in the end I found myself buying grommets and making top hats and stitching lace cuffs to Steampunk frock coats in preparation for my first-time convention experience. While there seemed to be no hard and fast rule regarding dressing the part when it came to attending a con for the first time, it seemed a rather momentous milestone, and I decided if I was in for a penny, I was in for a pound. I also knew that if I did not at least attempt to participate, I would spend the day wishing that I had. If my one time attending the Bay Area Renaissance Festival in street clothes taught me anything, it is that I hate participating half way.

I was, to be fair, no stranger to costuming, having spent thirteen years as a professional storyteller and acting on stage at various theatres and Renaissance Festivals. But finding myself suddenly free of the limits of Renaissance color and textiles and faux historical accuracy prescribed by the festival directors and the Society for Creative Anachronism, I decided to go all out and create a full Steampunk outfit, complete with brocaded frock coat, matching top hat, boots, corset, and watch chain. This activity consumed my evenings for several weeks and provided an excellent excuse to avoid editing my current manuscript. Finally, armed with a

coordinating decorative Victorian style wicker picnic hamper, copies of the then four books in my Steampunk series and (naturally) a parasol matching my costume, I climbed into the car with friends who were also exhibitors, and headed off into the sunrise (as it were), remembering the most important rule from my Renaissance Festival days—only wear the comfortable parts of the costume in the car!

On the way to the convention I found myself assailed by other Renaissance Festival memories—rising early in the morning on a day I would normally sleep in, gathering costume pieces, loading the car, meeting the others amid that strange juxtaposition of story and reality. Eating McDonald's in the back seat of the car dressed in at least half the accoutrements of a Victorian alt-history character from one of my novels, I found myself preparing to don a persona on the other side of the doors. In my Renaissance Festival days, I experienced the early morning hush of a secluded forest setting, half-timbered buildings, and colorful tents with flags snapping in the breeze. At the convention it was the echoing, half empty hall, slowly coming to life, gradually filling with vendors and exhibitors, the air of expectancy and excitement, and the hum and bustle of people preparing wares and costumes for the day. The pride of that little laminated badge, the cacophony of color and sound, the shrieks of laughter and cries of recognition as friends ran into each other, and that burst of happiness as a familiar face appeared unexpectedly out of the crowd. Old friends, new friends, and sitting in a quiet corner to step back for a moment and take it all in.

It was upon the actual public opening of the event, held in the Convention Center in downtown Tampa, that my original expectations and the reality of the convention experience actually met for the first time. I will admit it was not love at first sight. Wandering on my own (while the friends I had traveled with manned book booths and exhibitor tables), I found that the cacophony and clamor of the crowded convention hall was rather overwhelming. I felt out of place, miscast, as though I were an outsider attempting to infiltrate a culture about which in reality I knew very little. I was not a huge fan of any popular science fiction or fantasy franchises, I did not read comic books, had never played a video game in my life, and my understanding of Anime genre culture was limited to an irrational but exuberant appreciation for striped stockings and brightly colored wigs. I felt like an outsider.

This perception—which was entirely my own, and not based on interactions with anyone at the convention—lasted for the better part of an unfortunate hour, until I finally realized that in order to meet people, I would have to actually (wait for it…) meet people. The only thing keeping me apart from the thousands of people attending the convention was myself. Knowing that the current would simply pass me by if I did not leave the metaphorical river bank, I eventually jumped in and started swimming.

One of the things that surprised me and made a positive impact on my perception of not only this con but con culture as a whole, was the cosplay element inherent in the experience. I had expected cosplay, had prepared myself to be impressed, even intimidated by the level of workmanship and originality and talent I would see embodied in the cosplayers attending, but the diversity I experienced gave me a whole new appreciation for the convention experience. The costumes themselves ranged from the simple to the intricate, with some of the least intricate ensembles representing character concepts beautiful in their simplicity: An embodiment of Vincent Van Gogh characterized by a natural red beard, felt hat, tweed jacket, and painter's palette, and a movie-based interpretation of grown-up Christopher Robin with a raincoat, briefcase, stuffed bear, and red balloon, were simple but poignant portraits of icons with which we are all familiar, drawing the observer into the construct by means of shared experience. At the other end of the spectrum, detail perfect recreations of movie characters and comic book heroes and villains walked side by side with full body costumes, professional level movie makeup, and a fully articulated larger than life robot accompanied by a gear-and-goggle flaunting Steampunk engineer. Amid and among these, convention-goers flocked to booths and panels and exhibitor tables, wearing jeans and street clothes, franchise T-shirts, and theme-based dresses made from *Star Wars* or *Doctor Who* printed fabric.

Along with every level of costuming imaginable, there were all genders, ethnicities, and body types represented, as well as young and older and differently-abled. There seemed no limit to the creativity. As I sat for a brief respite at a courtyard table, to my left I saw the Three Musketeers chatting with a Josey Wales-era Clint Eastwood, while to my right, Disney's Belle and Elsa and Anna looked ready to burst into song. Behind them, a perfectly accessorized classic vampire waited, wide eyed and grinning, no more than six years old. The Guardians of the Galaxy were walking around in a group, squealing whenever they came across another character from their franchise, and incorporating them into the presentation (at first there was just Yondu, but by halfway through the morning there were Groot and Gamora and Rocket and Star Lord, too). The costumes ranged from store-bought, pre-made pieces to the hand-crafted and impossibly elaborate.

The level of creativity and imagination also brought the experience to a whole different level, as not all of the cosplayers limited themselves to a single character or interpretation. There was a Tyrannosaurus Rex dressed as Negan from the *Walking Dead*, and a full-on Hugh Jackman Greatest Showman with adamantium Wolverine claws. And Deadpools. So. Many. Deadpools. In a Terry Pratchett-esque moment, I saw the Grim Reaper exit the men's room with a scythe under one arm, drying his hands on a paper towel. Though creepy, I had to commend his commitment to personal hygiene. I, in short, was incredibly impressed and vastly entertained by the variety and creativity, and I spent half the morning posting pictures of it all on Facebook (for those of us of a certain vintage—the kind who need a nine-year-old to program the DVR—Instagram, Reddit, and Snapchat still fall under the category of "things the kids are doing these days." I make no apologies).

As the morning wore on, I explored the entirety of the vendor's hall, amazed by the variety and artistry of many of the exhibitors, relaxing into the experience, but still proceeding with a sort of tourist sensibility, observing politely, as though I were an outsider attempting to pass myself off as someone who "belonged." Halfway through the day, I decided to attend some panels, as the panel in which I was scheduled to participate would not occur until late afternoon. It was while sitting in panels on Steampunk costuming and persona that I found my perspective on conventions (and my presence at this one) altered by the words of one of the panel presenters. The series of panels (hosted by the Tampa Bay Steampunk Society) were interesting and informative, and—as do many similar steampunk panels—spoke a great deal about the maker movement. Though many elements of the maker movement focus on technology, it also represents a culture of hands on participatory artisan pursuits grounded in relevancy and innovation.

For me, hopeless with tools and more inclined toward Steampunk stories than Steampunk tech and machinery, the idea of a maker movement had always left me feeling outside of the bounds of a talented and fascinating group of individuals, with whom I could never hope to compare or connect. These panels, however, explored the Steampunk/maker movement not only as one of technology and machinery, but of persona, costuming, and character. The heart of the Steampunk costuming experience was shown in direct connection to the creative process of defining and subsequently portraying the character for whom that costume would be appropriate. Through this approach, cosplay in the Steampunk world becomes not presentational so much as participatory.

As an author, I had the sudden revelation that—in creating characters, settings, worlds, and stories (and costumes by extension)—I, too, was a part of this aspect of the maker movement, though in a different way than I had been envisioning. The speakers for this panel were passionate about their subject, accessible, and inclusive, and I loved their assertion that at its heart, Steampunk is not about the costume, but the story: That costuming is the second step and that the story should come first. The costumes act not merely as aesthetic representation, but as a means to tell that story. In that moment, my entire perspective altered.

In the light of that epiphany, I began to view costuming (at least in the Steampunk genre) as the building of a character in the same way one would for a book, including background, physicality, personality, and story arc. Viewing the creation, through costume, of a character is an incarnation of the storytelling process. According to this philosophy, by creating a character, and by extension using the  costume to interpret and represent that character, the makers become storytellers, and the storytellers become makers.

Once engaged in the experience of telling my story and portraying my character, I found myself feeling somewhat relieved that I had decided to go with a smaller, stylized top hat on a headband instead of a full-sized velvet one (a choice inspired by my desire to attempt a previously untried hat making method rather than using the hats I already had available).

Despite the gallant efforts of an industrial grade air conditioning system, it was hot in the convention hall, and I subsequently took frequent and necessary frock coat breaks to cool myself down. During one of these breaks, I found myself musing whether sweating in a costume qualified as suffering for one's art. If it does, I will confess to having been very artistic indeed.

As I rested, I took the time to observe the environment around me, the citizens of that environment, and how the convention itself created a shared experience, which in turn created a community—one with both its own culture and a connected but diverse population. The dichotomy of multiple fandoms, interests, and genres, and the shared passion of a large group of people gathered into one place to celebrate that passion, formed a microcosm of experience that, in all its diversity, still had more in common with its disparate participants than it had differences.

Though initially an outsider participating for the first time in an experience about which I knew virtually nothing, I found that within that shared experience there was a place for everyone: both the new and the seasoned, the beginner and the professional, the meticulously consummate and the casually curious. Spread across the floors and square footage of the convention center, a panoply of communities forged between them a greater whole, embracing the familiar, welcoming the stranger, and including not only the experienced and confident, but the cautious and the wary. I had entered into this community with the experience an unknown commodity, uncharted and without precedent, but before leaving the convention, I had found my place in the scheme of things. The need for this was intentional: I had entered into the experience with the goal of simple attendance and observation, but by the end of the day my perspective had shifted to a desire for immersion, for inclusion, for full participation as a member of this previously unfamiliar community.

The way in, for me, appeared where I should have already expected it, within the familiar architecture of my own experience. Participating in an author panel with three other Steampunk / alternate history authors, I found my way, in a sense, my confidence, the "character" to go with my costume, and in the end, being a member of that panel created an inhabitable space within the vast convention community, for a first-time visitor unsure of what to expect. Because here was something I did know. Something I had already lived. Something I knew how to share.

Participating on a Steampunk presentation panel with three other authors, I finally found my footing, allowing myself to feel a legitimate part of the convention experience, sharing my writing process, my personal and professional struggles and accomplishments, and most of all, the stories I had written. As an independent author, I spend most of my days making the books: writing them, formatting them, creating their covers, and then planning and outlining the next book. However, this day was less a day for creating the books and more about taking time to celebrate the books that were already published: Engaging with other authors about our work, discussing publishing and process, inspiration, and ideas, talking with audience members, encouraging others who wanted to write but were hesitant to try, created an entirely different experience than simply attending the convention as a member of the public. Across the conference room, we were faced with first time writers who looked at us in awe and admiration, little realizing that in the beginning, we too were first time writers; nervous, unsure, with nothing but stories and hopes in our hands.

We all spend our lives (whether at conventions or other settings) trying to find a place for ourselves, making our way, and hopefully finding success. As a guest speaker on that panel, I spoke confidently about my books, my writing process, and my future releases, yes. Yet earlier in the day I had attended the Steampunk costuming panel as an audience member, and I had spent the entire time mentally comparing my costume to the meticulous ensemble of one of the women conducting the panel—feeling hopelessly inadequate. Her Victorian ball gown was impossibly exquisite, incredibly elaborate, intimidatingly perfect, not to mention off-puttingly expensive to create. I'm pretty handy with ribbons and feathers—and I can create elaborate romantically embellished hats until the Victorian cows come home—but I could spend the rest of my life learning  to sew and I would still never be able to create something as stunning as the dress this woman was wearing. She was truly a gifted artist with a needle and thread. We all have our strengths and we all have our weaknesses: an artist with a needle I am not.

I realized that day that the hopeful writers attending the authors' panel looked at us with the same emotions of uncertainty and perceived inadequacy that I had felt looking at that professional costumer on the panel. Remembering exactly how that felt from my own beginning days as a writer, and my more recent experience attending the costuming panel, I talked with as many of the audience members as I could and encouraged them, assuring them that their processes were their own, that their dreams were important, and that their stories mattered. In that particular moment, making those connections with the audience attending the writer's panel, I suddenly realized that I, too, embodied the creative spirit of the process. In that moment, in my own medium of writing, I too was a maker.

The memory I think will stay with me forever was one shy young woman who talked with such trepidation and such longing about writing a book that I could feel her struggle from where I was sitting across the room. Throwing caution to the winds, I approached her after the panel. "Can I tell you something?" I asked her. "When you talk about writing a book, your entire face lights up. That tells me how important it is to you, how much you want to do it, and how likely you are to succeed because of that. Don't let doubt stop you from doing what you want to do." I gave her my email address, and urged her to take that first step, to write that first word, to imagine that first book and then make it a reality. I told her to email me if she had questions, hesitations, or simply needed encouragement as she began her writer/maker journey. I hope I hear from her. Not because I hope that she has questions or hesitations, but because I want to encourage and support her in the same way that I was encouraged and supported by several established authors when I was beginning.

Like my earliest forays into writing, attending my first convention was a strange experience stepping into a new, confusing, and wildly creative world, and I was grateful for the mentoring of friends and, as the saying goes, the kindness of strangers. As it happens, quite unexpectedly, between the beginning and the end of the convention, some of those strangers became friends.

Book One: For the Love of the Con

4 INTERNET FRIENDS ARE THE BEST FRIENDS
Joyce McGuire

I need to preface this by saying that prior to 2016, I had never been to any type of convention…save a couple of gun shows during my time in Mississippi, because when you're bored and dating a redneck in one of the most holier-than-thou-red-hell states in the union that's what you do on the weekends.

This honestly starts a few months before the glorious journey to the West coast, when I received a text message from a very, very good friend named Jon, whom I'd known online since I was 18 years old from our mutual nerdom love of wrestling. It said something to the effect of, "Hey, I think I may have won a trip…do you want to go?"

My natural inclination was to check my bank account before quickly firing off a return text of "FUCK YES, I DO!"

"Stay tuned--," was all he responded with.

Another couple of weeks passed before he got confirmation that he had indeed won an all-expenses paid trip to 2016's San Diego Comic-Con for himself and three friends through a service called Comic-Con HQ. It took another week of logistics planning…getting our IDs out to Comic HQ, getting travel booked from Seattle (where Jon lived) to San Diego, and getting our hotel reservations confirmed.

The only caveat for me in all of this? I lived in Sarasota, FL at the time and needed to get my behind to Seattle to fly out with the rest of them. Well, go big or go home, right? I booked my travel with little incident, even though it meant spending the night in the Seattle airport. Airports are never a comfortable place to sleep and I was too cheap to get a hotel room for just one night—so I found a bench and tried to crash for a few hours in between watching movies on my laptop. Keeping myself entertained has never been a problem.

Morning in the airport brought the arrival of Jon…and two of his friends.

Jon and I had known each other online for 12 years at that point.

We'd shared good times and bad. We'd been there for each other through thick and thin. Now, meeting him for the first time in person, I learned he gives great big bear hugs, I learned how rough his hands were from his chosen profession of being a marine carpenter, and most of all, I learned exactly much he hates flying. Suffice to say, he held my hand for a majority of the flight from Seattle to San Diego.

When we landed and got our bags, getting to our hotel and picking up our badges for all four days of SDCC was an adventure of its own.

Jon's winnings included flights, two hotel rooms, four-day tickets to SDCC, and tickets to the Her-Universe Fashion Show on Wednesday night. I must admit to being a party-pooper on Wednesday night and choosing to skip the fashion show because I'd been exhausted from traveling across the country and being awake for almost two days. Jon and his friends told me the show was amazing. And I also misjudged the Vikings panel time, thinking it was on Friday (hint hint-it wasn't-hint hint), but Jon was amazing and brought me back an official Vikings drinking horn that sits proudly on my knick-knack shelf to this day.

Keeping with the theme of my life, I slept as hard as possible in the hotel room I shared with Jon in order to be as ready as possible for the next day. That, and our first night's dinner was at Dick's Last Resort...which is unfortunately closed now. Jon and friends were very amused with  how rude the waitstaff was, which as you know, is the entire appeal of an establishment like Dick's...besides the great cocktail choices.

Now, I had been to San Diego before. I knew my general way around the area of the Convention Center thanks to a business trip a few years prior, but nothing really prepares you for the utter majesty of your first real comic convention. It feels like 100,000 plus like-minded people descend upon San Diego for this amazing holy-land experience of nerdom.

The first morning in the hotel came with free hot breakfast and even hotter coffee. Jon and I took the time each morning we were there to indulge and talk about our plan of attack for the day. (We never really stuck to the plan. If something got in the way or we found something that was absolutely amazing, we had smartphones. We could just call or text each other!)

When I was able to pick my jaw up off the floor after gaping at just how *big* the whole of the convention center and everything they jam pack in there really is…I set off to explore.

My first day at San Diego Comic-Con was utterly magical. The sheer number of things to see is almost mind-boggling. People in all sorts of amazing cosplays, big company booths, and displays of toys/comics/movies. There were independent artists and authors as far as the eye could see and all the fandom merchandise one could hope to purchase in a lifetime. It was midday on Thursday after we got to walking around that I separated from Jon and his friends to do some exploring on my own.

Jon and his friends are the type to take four days to look at every little thing, which is absolutely their right...I'm just the type to blitz an area to see what's all there before making a second trip to look more in-depth at the things I really want to see. It helps me gauge where my time should really be spent. Having never been to any type of convention before, I had very little idea as to what to expect...

But the first day—at least for a couple of hours—we all stuck together, and I got to see my very first panel! It was for a group called Critical Role that Jon and his friends were really into. For those of you that don't know (I certainly didn't know!), Critical Role is essentially a web series usually broadcast on Twitch or YouTube of a group of professional voice actors that play Dungeons and Dragons. Even having no idea who these people were, it was fun to watch the  panel and get a more in-depth look as to how such a thing worked. Not to mention, Jon was all smiles; which made me all smiles. Seeing my friends happy is something that gives me no end of joy.

We had a blast just sitting down and watching the events they put on there every day. We lingered at the Comic-Con HQ area exploring the convention's offerings. Comic-Con HQ provided a lot of free swag every day, not to mention the low-cost drinks...and comfortable places to sit with electrical outlets so you could recharge your phone, the importance of which cannot be overstated when you spend the majority of your day taking pictures of *everything* for everyone you know who might remotely like a thing you see...and killing your phone battery in the process.

It was comfortable to have a routine while I was out there though.

Jon and friends were usually up a little earlier than me, but Jon was a sweetheart and woke me up, so we could have breakfast together each day. Then, it was back to the hotel room to shower and get on the shuttles to take us to the convention center to begin another day of amazing sight-seeing. Thursday and Friday were honestly the best days for just exploring and seeing what I could, because remotely trying to get close to anything on Saturday was nigh on impossible. The crowds seemed to double over the weekend and getting up close to anything was a long line followed by a longer line. It was frustrating at first, but with Saturday came the sudden realization of being free to do whatever I wanted now because I had spent the majority of Thursday and Friday seeing all of the booths and artists I had wanted to see. That included the artist and writer of two webcomics I've followed for the better part of a decade called *Looking For Group* and *Least I Could Do*. I started following these comics around 2006 and despite some lapses, the art is very good and the storylines are amusing. *Looking for Group* is my absolute favorite of the two as it is a comedy high-fantasy series. It was thrilling to get a few moments with the creators to tell them how much I admired their work and to grab a photo of them!

With the influx of people making it ridiculously hard to get around, the next part of my adventure was going on a scavenger hunt for things my friends—online and back home—wanted. One of them, from Upstate New York, was looking for the Shockmaster toy that had been released. For those of you curious as to what the hell a Shockmaster is: in the early 90s wrestling world, a wrestler named Fred Ottman (most famously known as Tugboat and Typhoon) debuted in World Championship Wrestling (WCW) as a character in a silver sparkly Stormtrooper mask as The Shockmaster and it is regarded as one of the single worst debuts in wrestling history (he fell over and broke his mask). Even the San Diego Comic Con-exclusive toy has him upside down and backwards in the packaging, as you can see modeled by Jon here.

I stood in line for almost an hour to get this toy for my friend and when a few others heard what I had done for my friend in Upstate New York, I began to get requests for other things. My friend Ross in Indiana was looking for one of the Funko Pops of the "Help It's the Hair Bear Bunch!" for his wife, as the cartoon was one of her favorites as a child. That was considerably harder to get as, in my search for one, I discovered that every morning, there was a lottery held to be able to actually shop at the Funko Pop booth and you couldn't just hop in line to get the one you wanted. So, it took a bit of ingenuity and bribery to get that. I promised a person in line an extra ten dollars if they would get me one of the toys...and it actually worked! Ross and my friend from Upstate New York were thrilled to get their treasures mailed to them a few days after I got home.

My friend Robyn is an enormous fan of mermaids and thus, obtaining an original print of the famous *Little Mermaid* illustration by

J. Scott Campbell for her was the highlight of her summer. Another friend of mine asked for a print by an artist who has done incredible work for Marvel and DC comics. I was lucky enough to stop by his booth while he was there to get his print signed...only to find out that he is not the most pleasant person in the world. Perhaps he was just having an off day, but I stood there for ten minutes waiting just to be acknowledged before his assistant prodded him to sign the print and well, it got tossed back to me like so much garbage. He might be an incredible artist, but on that day, he was just a rude asshole.

It didn't sour my opinion of the convention in the slightest though.

Hunting for these treasures for just downright *fun*. In the midst of my hunt for merch, I ventured to several of the outside exhibits...one of which was the amazingly horrific furniture displays from the upcoming season of *American Horror Story: Hotel* (2015). There was also a huge replica of the statue of Superman from *Batman vs. Superman* (2013), as well as a replica of the Batmobile from that movie. In the midst of seeing all of these things, I ended up in a line.

When it comes right down to it, most of your San Diego Comic-Con experience is waiting in a line for something. This line ended up being for some free con swag of your choice...the best choice being a replica Wonder Woman tiara that I unashamedly wore for the rest of the day along with the rest of the fans—young and old—who also decided the Wonder Woman tiara was their jam.

It was my first tiny piece of cosplay.

I've indulged in a few more pieces since that day, to say the least. San Diego Comic-Con is definitely the mecca of amazing cosplayers. When I needed a moment to rest, there's no understating the joy that I got just from sitting in some random spot and watching all of these amazing people who put so much time and energy into these costumes of characters they loved. A few of my favorites were the gazillion Loki cosplayers (I'm an unashamed Loki-fangirl. Always have been, always will be!), a pair of best friends who'd dressed up as Thor and Loki, the most incredible Spider-Gwen I've ever seen, a beautiful vintage Catwoman, and the one who went viral: the Ronald McDonald-Thor. Not to mention, the mother I met in the Comic-

Con HQ who dressed up as a *perfect* rendition of Narcissa Malfoy from the *Harry Potter* movies. I let out the most undignified squeal when I saw her and rushed over to ask if I could get a picture of her. She just laughed at my response and told me that I could absolutely take her picture, I took a dozen of her alone!

As Saturday came to a close, Jon and I shared a great dinner that was literally across the street from the convention center...and my memory sucks so I don't actually remember what we had. We parted after dinner. I went back to the hotel room because I was exhausted. Jon and his friends had decided to camp out overnight in the line for Hall H to catch the *Supernatural* panel first thing in the morning on Sunday. *Supernatural* is a great show, but I've never really been into it. I did make sure to give the guys my extra battery banks to keep their cell phones charged (while they killed time overnight). It was incredible to see a lot of people's dedication to seeing that panel, and how prepared they were to wait overnight to get into the hall: They came with solar panels to charge their devices, some had tents, and others had camping chairs.

What sticks in my mind more was this amazing experience and spending time with one of my favorite people, whom I had finally gotten to meet in person after knowing them for more than a decade online. You know you have really great friends when they give you opportunity to share in an experience like a free trip to San Diego Comic-Con. We've had our differences over the years, but we've remained close.

I can't thank him enough for inviting me along.

Someday I'll make the trek out West again to attend another convention with him, but next time, I'm going to stock up on the antibiotics because San Diego Comic-Con's final parting gift to me was a wicked case of con-flu that turned into an upper respiratory infection. The only warning I got about that was *after* I got back home.

San Diego Comic-Con was my first. It sure as hell won't be my last.

Book One: For the Love of the Con

PART TWO
FOR THE LOVE OF THE CON

Book One: For the Love of the Con

5 TAKING OVER THE WHOLE LIBRARY[1]
Valerie Estelle Frankel

I have never seen so many people in a library in my life. I watch from my table as the clock turns to 10:00 am. Dozens of teen volunteers in special shirts stand waiting, having warmed up with doughnuts and a giant stack of water bottles. The doors open and a mob swarms into Santa Clara Library's annual comic-con, most everyone under the age of ten.

The kids are instantly captivated. How not? An old style Cylon (do kids know that one?) along with BB-8 and Admiral Ackbar statues greet them in the lobby. There's not just one working R2-D2 but a swarm of them. There are Stormtroopers, bounty hunters, Vader, and a very credible Leia, a Rey, and a Windu: Three *Star Wars* costume groups are here, hamming it up. There's also a set of Disney princesses in giant ballgowns.  Spiderman and an impressive Doctor Doom wander around as well.

---

[1] Note: Everyone quoted here is a friend of Valerie Frankel and has given us full permission to be quoted within the context of this chapter.

Book One: For the Love of the Con

Everyone's happy to pose for photos (though they unfortunately keep stopping in the aisles). Costumers, both officially invited and off the street, are high-fiving the kids and cracking jokes—part of the impromptu entertainment. No one's afraid of Vader, and even the giant guts monster doesn't evoke many whimpers from the little ones. Vader breathes deeply through the mask and then says in a sonorous but friendly voice, "Hi Batgirl" to a child in a sparkly costume. "Does anyone have the time?" he asks formally. I tell him, and he actually lets out a very human yelp. "Really? I'm late for story time." He turns to the excellent Rey he's been posing with. "You too?"

No, as it happens, she's just there for fun.

While this is a library event, it does all it can to hit all the convention perks. There's registration (free tickets through Eventbrite) with official-looking badges. The walls are covered in simple superhero decorations and *Star Wars* decals. Someone has picked up freebees and posters from the "real" San Diego Comic-Con to pass out, as well as some of the giant foam hands used to publicize the kiddie cartoon *Marvel Rising*. Game Kastle, a local comics and games shop, has taken over half a floor—and they're not just selling games but running them on the tables. Another convention has sent anime screenings. Hidden by the programming area is an entire additional shopping room with lots of themed Legos and toys.

When I first discovered this event was coming, I eagerly volunteered my services as a guest author. The library staff were kind enough to supply a free table (something that can run $50 to $100 at a fan-run convention, and $300 or much more at a more commercial comic con). I rounded up a few of my author friends to provide an entire table of "real Silicon Valley authors" and we were off. (Sharing tables is wonderful, not only to split the costs but the labor. With enough people around, we can even attend convention events. More on that later.) This is the third year I've returned for it, as each has been an eagerly-anticipated success.

In the main lobby, the artist's alley with local writers and artists (myself included) gets busy selling books and handing out their own freebees. The library provides a catered lunch for us and the volunteers—a lovely touch. Of course, the volunteers taking the food orders really have to squeeze around as the throng of kids and adults crowd the limited hall space. Weapons are allowed, but not "real weapons"—to be fair, there are no incidents with the plastic laser guns and lightsabers. That's quite a feat considering how mobbed the place is.

The entire library has been taken over—certainly the program room and children's section but also the entire adult nonfiction floor upstairs. That's quite a stunt for an average Saturday in October, with the library remaining open. Books and computers for ordinary library-goers are still available, but one has to inch around the noisy crafting and game-playing children. All the upstairs tables have been converted into craft space. It's a limited space, but the event planners are making the most of it, while still keeping the printers available (as I found out in my own quick scramble for an accounts sheet).

Additional parking would be nice too, as we spilled into the neighboring lots and then finally across the street.

Outside, local Ghostbusters show off their car, opposite a souped-up DeLorean (around the Bay Area, a *Jurassic Park* jeep also makes the rounds). When they've already built such a cool toy, their bringing it around for people to adore is easy to arrange. There are food trucks and a big water truck too. Leaping on board with the actual library part, discount books are on sale by the door. In the park behind the library there are tents with cotton candy and giveaways. Of course, the Bookmobile is parked here too. In one tent, the Department of Public Works has sent forth a group of actual superheroines in matching t-shirts and capes to represent their lofty goals and advertise their city-sponsored clean-up project, even while actually picking up trash around the event. Clearly, they're getting into the spirit with official city works.

Most popular is a large roped-off area with a special tent and tables. Kids who go in get to decorate a Captain American paper plate shield, Yoda paper bag puppets, and so on from simple kits. Putting duct tape stickers on chopped up pool noodles to make lightsabers is the most popular, and there's an event teaching the kids how to duel with them after.

Inside at the authors' and artists' tables, the crowds aren't necessarily buying much—the kids don't have cash and the adults think they should be happy with all the freebees. The majority of adults, in fact, seem to be there escorting children. Still, the sellers tend to be fans. Dave M. Strom, author of the humorous Super-Holly series, comments, "I bought a graphic novel or two and some comic books. All indie stuff, do not expect Marvel Comics actors there. Expect the little guy, the indie artists, and be inspired to say, 'Hey, I can try this too!'" My friend and fellow seller author C. Stanford Lowe consoles herself that at least she gets a lovely catered lunch, and points out how much fun the event is, even with weak sales. As she adds, "I love the young energy. The high school helpers were so high energy, taking pictures and posing up and down the aisles. Wonderful costumes." As she and I agree, it's clearly "a fabulous idea to get people into the libraries."

Little comic-cons are springing up everywhere: at community centers, at colleges, and now in libraries. One must assume the proliferation of so many is echoing the world of science fiction going mainstream. Comic-Con is famous now, with all the movie stars' panels hitting YouTube. Likewise, *Doctor Who, Star Wars* and superheroes have been rebooted for the newest generation, soaring to immense popularity. As kids and teens embrace it all, they want to join in the fun. Since they can't cross the country to attend these expensive pro comic-cons without a very indulgent parent, smaller local conventions give them an alternative.

Of course, as comic-cons go, there's little at the library comic-con to attract the "grown-ups" if they aren't there with kids or performing for them. My dad, who'd been working with the city to upgrade the library's technology, arrived in his full Jedi regalia and "real" lightsaber. (Yes, the pair of us attend many conventions together—me for the bookselling and him for the costuming. And, yes, I'm wearing foam bagels.) On his arrival, he took a few photos, let kids try his lightsaber, and finally headed home after an hour since the advertised lightsaber-dueling event was with Styrofoam—and kid-centric. All the activities, he found, were really meant for a young audience. He described the con afterwards as "very nicely done but child-oriented. Great place for a family to go." Still, he didn't find much to entertain an enthusiastic adult. Likewise, another friend expressed disappointment in missing the con but added that there was no way he was planning to be up at ten on a weekend morning. When I explained why there were no night activities, and in fact, what the day activities had covered, his disappointment quickly turned to relief.

My fellow author, Sandra Saidak, also describes problems with the bookshelves being in the way amidst the massive crowd and adds, "Trying to navigate the way around the library—you had to learn your routes." Weaving through the maze of hidden corners, her most delightful moment is discovering a pair of Stormtroopers waving people through. "Since when have you been doing security?" she asks.

"Oh, since they blew up the Death Star," one replies without a pause.

Of course, the fans are happy to provide entertainment of their own. Inviting the local 501st Legion means very popular booths, gadgets, and displays. In fact, the photo booth has "celebrities" like R2-D2 or a trio of Disney Princesses posing with the kids at scheduled times. Exhibits scattered in corners of the library include a Gunpla Build Contest and team trivia. On the sidewalk, a volunteer has sketched Superman and Captain Marvel's emblems in  colorful chalk, and then left the rest for the kids to design. More complex stations have kids fashion cut up comic pages into decorations for water bottles and button making. They also get to make comic-covered pop sockets and outlet covers as well as actual pop-up comic books. A more original set of tables in the kids' area teach how to construct a red paper bow tie…and add an LED in the center to make it glow. As the day goes on, all the kids have these glowing bows, setting off their foam lightsabers and paper Pikachu ears.

The head librarian and assistant librarian are both here checking out their handiwork. (In fact, two rooms were rushed to get the sound systems ready by the event.) In fact, the technology ends up working perfectly…it is Silicon Valley, after all. Some of the panels are particularly interactive. They kick off with a quick draw for kids. After this, Game Kastle shows kids how to paint gaming miniatures—undoubtedly useful for them as it promotes sales, but interesting for the kids as well. Other panels follow with everyone sharing their expertise—mostly about cosplay and drawing. Obviously, devoted fans who spend all day doing this anyway make energetic speakers on the topics. There are drawing demos out at the Bookmobile too. Lightsaber training (presumably kids whacking each other with the pool noodles until they tire) takes place outside. At his own panel, the local Captain Jack Sparrow cosplayer leads everyone in talking like a pirate amid goofy laughter. There are also the professional writers, artists, and even cosplayers (since one suspects being Captain Jack even at birthday parties likely isn't a full-time gig). The kids are clearly having an amazing time. As a friend points out to me, the three-year-olds don't realize it's not really Spider-Man. And the R2-D2s are as real as it gets.

Tiny stations offer readings, signings, and autographs by local authors, including some impressive talent. Graphic novelists Ru Xu

(*NewsPrints*) and Nidhi Chanani (*Pashmina*) give a talk on making comics for kids. The Walt Disney Family Museum Studio Team also share their techniques from art to story structure. Ben Costa & James Parks, the illustrator and writer of the graphic novel series *Rickety Stitch,* teach kids to create their own comics. Kaitlyn Dias, voice of Riley in Pixar's *Inside Out,* is signing, as is Genevieve Santos, illustrator of *Daisy Dreamer.* After this, "Animator and visual effects artist Webster Colcord takes us behind-the-scenes of animation and visual effects projects that he has worked on for studios such as Fox, Disney, DreamWorks, and Nickelodeon," as the program explains. Tickets are required for this, but they're free, and the line isn't even too bad. The day finishes with another ticketed event—behind the scenes details from the new anime-style cartoon *Star Wars Resistance.* Joel Aron (Director of Cinematography) and Keith Kellogg (Animation Supervisor) are the star attraction, saved up for 2:30 and 3:30pm to close out the afternoon.

Author Dave M. Strom adds that in navigating the place, he kept running into "narrow aisles, lots of people, and usually at least one person in a way-oversized costume like a giant hoop skirt or a huge alien/demon four-foot-wide-shoulders plastic or papier-mâché home built tribute to some anime I have never heard of." Certainly, my running upstairs to check out the activities or grab sandwiches feels like being a salmon swimming upstream. Everyone's friendly, but some costumes really block a wide space bubble, even before everyone bottlenecks to take photos. As Strom concludes: "For such a small con, it has a little feel of a larger crowded one: lots of bodies, lots of cosplay. (I know of what I speak, I have been to the San Diego Comic-Con when they did not have crowd control.)...This is a friendly little comic con but be prepared to squeeze past people. Oh, and talk to a few of the artists and writers. And artistic writers."

I've seen other libraries try creative hooks for kids. Another, smaller, library comic-con had kids vote off between two superheroes each day in a "duel." On the last day, anyone dressed as Wonder Woman (as I was) or Black Panther got a free book. (They all appeared to be free samples sent to the library, as were the stack of free comic books out in front.) Other libraries, like the San Mateo Main Branch, Los Gatos Library, and San Jose Public Library, invite  local authors for a sign off, in the program room with readings or perhaps even on the lawn. San Mateo in particular devotes one day to comic artists, and then invites the local branch of California Writers Club to fill a room with signings and readings. Fremont Library does the same. Some libraries do a *Harry Potter* or superhero-themed escape room...often with a stack of atlases or kids' books on Roman numerals lying about in which everyone can find the answers to the puzzles. Others add crafts and activities for Free Comic Book Day in May. Certainly, many local celebrities are happy to come show off.

Likewise, Burlingame Main Library gave over its entire building to a *Harry Potter* Winter Ball after hours—cardboard candles from the ceiling, costumed librarians (and guests!), fortune telling, photo booth, face painting, themed bingo, author signings, props, scavenger hunt, dance party with disco ball, and so on. Teen volunteers decorated the top floor stacks with trees made of brown crumpled paper grocery bags to suggest the Forbidden Forest...and venturing in deep turned up a huge inflatable spider! Kids made golden snitches, wands, and owl puppets. The bathroom, complete with Moaning Myrtle sounds, was labeled Room of Requirement. The kids had a blast—spurred of course by free butterbeer and Potter-themed sugar cookies. Basically, a library is already a magical space, but with creativity and directions it can become so much more.

Of course, the library comic-con doesn't make a perfect day for everyone. As I'm scurrying about, I bump into a bewildered eighty-year-old acquaintance who didn't expect all this and had only come in to use the computer. I assure her the library is still functioning (I have in fact checked out my usual stack of books and even frantically made copies.). Still, I can imagine the entire library's being taken over is quite a surprise for some. An upstairs librarian looks pained, as if he took the job for the quiet and now all his worst fears are invading. Indeed, it's noisy—the R2D2s beep and burble and shriek. Toddlers have meltdowns. Kids whack each other with lightsabers. Some costumes blast music until the walls seem to shake. But as a con for kids, it definitely does its job.

Sales this year haven't been great—my children's books are for older readers, and the little kids really seem to be here for the crafts and spectacle. Still, like all my author friends, I've found it a fun day out, to be in costume and celebrate the descent into geekery. Further, showing off our products and proclaiming our appearance on social media is always a plus, and I've given away some free eBooks for kids. The energy filling the space is incredible, even for a lifelong library lover like myself. In the same way that self-publishing has opened up the industry to anyone with a good idea and the will to write it, the popularity of comic-cons has inspired convention centers, libraries, and even schools to throw some Spider-Man decals on the walls, assemble craft tables, and line up a few Darth Vaders and Cinderellas to lead Storytime. Some of the attending children may take inspiration from the *Star Wars* Resistance panel to draw their own cartoons or someday produce television. Others will simply dump their Supergirl costumes and new lightsabers back in the closet. But even for those who don't spend much time at libraries, it's a reminder that these places offer a world of imagination meant for everyone, not just those with the means to attend the big conventions.

6 BADGES OF HONOR
Marci Bretts

"Name?"

"Marci Bretts. I pre-registered."

"Badge name?"

"Cat Whisperer."

Badges are typically used at cons to serve as physical signs of paid admission, but they represent far more than a name badge. At all cons they are an obvious sign of attending, a simple way to distinguish attendees from the "muggles" who may be using the same location for their own, mundane purposes. Pop-culture conventions create an atmosphere to entice people to attend a paid event, one that offers acceptance and entertainment, camaraderie and validation, knowledge and opportunity. To create this environment, organizers use methods that seem simple or obvious but have deeper meanings to attendees and fans, meanings and influence that may be unconscious to attendees.

Convention organizers use the simple terms "membership," "badge," and other such words in regard to the selling of convention tickets and marketing of cons to both self-identified fans (geeks or nerds) and to the general populace. The beliefs behind simple words and concepts such as "membership" and "badge" include those of inclusivity and exclusivity, and they influence attendees and fans in ways that may not be consciously apparent to those acting on these beliefs. These words have concrete and surface meanings that are understood by all, but I will be addressing more of the atmosphere that these words create and their influence on fans' feelings and behaviors. I will be exploring the use of those and other words used by convention organizers, either by habit or on purpose to influence new and potential attendees.

Beyond words, the marketing and statements used by both organizers and attendees create the temporary space in which both groups operate. Sometimes it is difficult to ascertain who exactly runs the events and whether control over anticipated and desired content is determined more with the attendees than with the organizers. Organizers may set a schedule and determine the location  and appearance of certain persons, but all cons to some extent have their atmosphere set by the attendees, who determine the tone simply by their overwhelming numbers.

Membership and science fiction/fantasy have a long history. Science fiction and fantasy fan groups have been around since the 1930s and quickly moved from informal gatherings to formal, organized groups with membership rolls, newsletters and magazines and then organized events like conferences. Money was crucial to keeping these groups running, as there were newsletters to be printed and mailed, facilities to be rented for special events, and franchise fees to fan club organizations, so charging for memberships was one way to cover costs. Events such as parties, large meetings, or conferences with presenters necessitated a fee to attend, but as with other social clubs, members in good standing were entitled to participate in the decisions surrounding such events. Then, as now, these clubs or groups had a formal structure that involved officers, written rules and procedures, and paid members could at least voice their opinion and often vote on major decisions.

So, what is the modern relationship of an attendee to con organizations? An attendee purchases a ticket, which at the very least includes admission to a convention. But it may also be called a badge or sometimes a membership. Modern conventions may use the term "ticket" to sell admission to their events, but the idea of membership remains as a concept on everyone's mind, so much so that the term "membership" is often used, particularly at fan-run conventions or those that call themselves "fan-forward," regardless of their non-profit or for-profit tax status. WorldCon, Otakon, LosCon, and other cons use the term to refer to tickets to a convention. I've long wondered about the formal and informal use of the term; at first glance it doesn't make sense. What does a membership have to do with going to a meeting of the geeks? What does an attendee obtain from such a purchase, other than admission to an event? And what does it mean to the attendee? Do I even want to be a member of this club?

The term "membership" carries a lot of meaning that attendees may not be consciously considering. Membership: to belong to a selective group. Membership: to be included and accepted. This is particularly special for a group of people who have been historically marginalized and may have very well been ostracized in their own lives. While I've been a nerd or a geek my whole life, it's been a relatively recent phenomenon to have literally hundreds of thousands join me at those organized events now called pop culture or multi-genre conventions, what longtime attendees call "cons" that cater to every obscure and not so obscure fandom of any and all media.

When I started going to cons, they were smaller events and most were organized by other fans for the primary purposes of enjoyment, enlightenment, and face to face meeting and connecting with other geeks. Even the few for-profit conventions, such as those run by Creation Entertainment, were small enough to fit all the attendees into one hotel ballroom for their single-track programming that was heavy on celebrity appearances and sponsored vendors but short on variety. They were organized around a single fandom, which helped facilitate the shared belief system and fostered the group experience.

At the same time, multigenre and multimedia cons were run by nonprofits and their relatively small size (from 300 to 1500 attendees) facilitated interpersonal interactions and shared experiences. When I attended these, I would see the same people over and over in panels or a con suite. Multiply that over a weekend and at multiple conventions held over a year and it was inevitable that friendships—or at least a sense of shared purpose—would develop.

The recurrence of familiar faces continued as the conventions got larger and tens of thousands of people became accustomed to attending conventions. And cons became big business as geek culture became more mainstream.

This sense of community is quite similar to anyone who has willfully joined a group or a club for any specific interest or hobby. Just like the early science fiction fan groups, convention fans develop a sense of belonging from shared experiences and repeated contact with one another.

Now, add in the word "membership" to an event and most con-goers won't think twice about it. In fact, it may be a welcome idea. Why yes, I'm a member of that group who goes to cons, talks about geeky ideas, and may have "odd ideas" about what's important. So, what does membership to a con get me?

- Entry to a con, at least entry to a few rooms or events affiliated with a con
- A spiffy badge, often with a nickname of my own choosing
- ???? Yeah, not much else.

Do I get to vote on what topics will be addressed at a con? Guests to be invited? Fandoms to be included for consideration? Activities such as performances, games, social events? The answer to all of these questions is a qualified "no." Organizers may solicit topics or panel ideas, guest requests, and provide overall feedback on a con at the end of such an event, but the organizers are under no legal or even moral obligation to act on such requests. There is certainly a *financial* motivation to give fans what they want to see and do at a con, as fan service is a short way to a fan's wallet. It makes sense: Offer the fans what they want (or what an organizer thinks they want) and you get fan loyalty, repeat customers, and convention favoritism. Which leads to...feelings of membership to a group: A group, in this case, consisting of anyone who attends the same con as you and whom you see year after year. Oddly, this sense of loyalty is transferred more to the convention itself—that event that occurs in a particular city—than the real people running the event.

Conventions willfully use an attendee's desire for fandom authenticity through liberal use of the word "fan" in their marketing and outreach materials. They call themselves fan-forward (Dragon Con), fan-focused (MISTI-Con), and fan-first (Walker Stalker). Now, several (ironically, for-profit cons) use the word "fan" in their name, such as Fan Expo or FanFest (Phoenix,) FanX (Salt Lake Comic Convention), etc. While several of these cons are for-profit, most attendees will prefer to think their favorite con is run by fans with no profit motive and will ignore any signs that contradict that myth. The myth is useful to bolster an attendee's sense of loyalty, since a fan would be more likely to support a group of fans rather than a company that exists to profit off of them.

Membership through ticket purchase is an easy way to gain at least physical and hopefully conceptual entry to a group. The badge is a fast ticket to an inclusive club, available to those have felt excluded for a long time but still have that innate need to belong. The con provides validation for the person who has little support at home, school, or work, or in their other face-to-face interactions in real life. It provides a sense of community, at least for a few days, a shared cauldron of knowledge or excitement about topics and interests that has been simmering for months in preparation of consumption by an appreciative group.

But is this club or community an artificially created one, devoid of real emotional connections amongst the members? Community can be created simply from the sheer size of a group: larger groups giving greater feelings of identity but also making each individual's experience less personal. A fan's interests are reflected in those around her, visually reinforcing beliefs and transforming them from the imagined to the real.

While purchasing a ticket or badge is an obvious way to gain entry, I have taken the harder way to join such clubs or groups: I have become both a day and staff level volunteer at most of the cons I attend. At this point, I find it difficult to "just" go to a con as a "regular" attendee. Fortunately, or not, due to my multi-con volunteer status, I am volunteering year-round either for the events I help organize or those I attend while volunteering for another. Thus, for me, membership or inclusion in a group is included and dependent upon my active participation in the organizing or labor

associated with a con. Depending on the structure of the organization, I may enjoy the privileges commonly associated with membership and have some influence over parts of the convention. Or, I may only be able to put my mark on my own specific area of influence.

The use of the term "badge" should be obvious, in the sense that physical badges are issued to attendees to display as proof of their purchase to gain entry to the physical spaces of a con. But "badge" has other meanings or uses, such as to recognize the achievement of a skill or experience. Badges are then status symbols, put on display so that others may acknowledge the special status of the wearer and to convey a sense of honor. When such badges are extra difficult to obtain, such as those from cons that consistently sell-out like San Diego Comic-Con, the recipient of such badges proudly displays his/her/their badge with friends on social media and keep them as souvenirs after the event is long over. Even badges that are readily bought can become a collectible item for a loyal attendee.

Most cons will go to some lengths to make their badges distinctive. Organizers will create new designs for each year, some solicit or hire artists to create graphics. During registration, convention or badge names further individualize an otherwise impersonal badge. But some attendees take that personalization further. They alter the badge with stickers, pins and drawings to make the boring and impersonal the exciting and unique.

The con badges frequently become the attendees' personal superhero symbol. The badges may look the same except for the name, but of course that's not true. Badge names, stickers, pins, special lanyards...attendees take more than a casual view of their identity to other congoers. For those who aren't cosplaying, a badge can be a window into someone's not so secret identity, an identity possibly only let out during cons, one of the few places where a closet nerd can feel safe.

But if an attendee decorates a badge in order to stand out as an individual, the badges instead become a beacon to belong to yet more groups. The various symbols affixed to a badge or lanyard are there to declare one's loyalties to whatever brand of fiction holds sway over the bulk of the fan's dreams and aspirations. The logos, already themselves a shortcut to the stories they reference, become a second set of shortcuts to a set of beliefs and attitudes held by the bearer. Declaring an allegiance to a tribe of gamers or readers  provides a means to join the group or tribe of like-minded folks. For those who may have trouble meeting or talking to others, it provides an easier way to start a conversation.

Does the attendee get a more satisfying experience from gaining "membership" to a con, as opposed to merely obtaining a ticket? The returning attendee goes to the expense and emotional rollercoaster associated with vying with thousands of others to purchase a badge to an event that has become valuable to their sense of self. In return—for enduring the stress of sleepless nights, scavenging for hotel rooms, swapping codes with strangers, extensive prayers and gifts to the purchasing deities—the attendee is rewarded with a trip to "Nerdmas"/"Nerdi Gras" and inclusion to one of the most selective groups possible in the pop culture world. The accomplishment of a successful ticket purchase is now part of someone's personal history and the boost of confidence can't be measured by any objective means. In return for going to emotional, logistical and financial extremes to obtain limited numbers of badges and affordable accommodations, the attendee is rewarded with a trip to Nerd Paradise and inclusion to one of the most sought-after groups possible in the pop culture world: pop culture convention attendee. Bragging rights for a lifetime.

7 FUN AND GAMES WITH CON CELEBRITIES
Kathy Lockwood

Of course, since I've been to many conventions over the years, I've had a lot of experiences with the guest celebrities. Most have been awesome. The original *Star Trek* and *Battlestar Galactica* casts were amazing, for example. But there have been some particularly funny and not always positive experiences as well. So, I thought I would share a few of these here.

Nathan Fillion is Pissed at Me

After finishing my first master's thesis, which involved attending Dragon Con repeatedly to do my research, I was pretty over conventions for a while. Especially Dragon Con. Mind you, it's an awesome con, and I had been going for years, but it was getting so huge that it was starting to become more trouble than it was worth, especially since I had to travel there from Florida. Also, this was back around 2008 when celebrities had started charging for everything. $25 for an autograph. $25 for a photo to sign. $50 for a photo op (no pro photographer, just whoever was willing to take the picture for you). It was getting really ridiculous, as I don't understand why I have to pay them so much when they make more money than I do in a year just by walking on set.

The reason I was at Dragon Con yet again that year was because a couple of close friends were going. Plus, most of the cast of *Firefly/Serenity* would be there, along with some folks from the *Battlestar Galactica* reboot and *Heroes*. I am a huge fan of all those, and my son was not only a big *Heroes* and *Firefly* fan, but he specifically dug actor Alan Tudyk and his character "Wash" Washburne. In fact, my son's gamer tag was—and still is—Washii or variations thereof. I'll have to admit he was my favorite character too.

So, we decided to make the trek to Dragon Con yet again since there were so many celebrities we wanted to meet. On the down side, we didn't want to spend the kind of money it would take to meet them all. In fact, at one point, I started blowing off people based on their "price." That and the principle of the thing. All the aforementioned productions were fairly recent at that time, so it wasn't like running into some poor starving actor decades after he was famous who hasn't worked since. (On a quick related side note: kudos and serious LOLs to Tudyk and his web series *Con Man*. If you haven't seen it, it ties into my last comment. And you should totally just see it.)

So, we were standing in line to see several actors at this one table, including Tudyk and Nathan Fillion. There were signs up telling people not to take pictures. This used to be a rule back when people used cameras more, because the actors didn't want flashes in their faces all day. Who could blame them? But at that time, digital cameras had come out, so it was possible to take decent pictures without using the flash. But that flew in the face of the new reason they weren't allowed: because the actors wanted to charge a boatload of money for you to take that picture—even if it was a random shot from a distance that would probably turn out to be an unidentifiable top of a head as the person signed autographs.

Well, being rather annoyed at this whole situation, and being a couple of rows back in a long and winding line, I decided I was going  to take a darn picture if the chance presented itself, and it did. I got to a point when I noticed there was an opening in the line where I had a brief but clear view of Fillion. Yes, he had his head down signing things and I'd probably end up with a lousy pic, but whatever. I had already dropped some major cash for a signed photo and really didn't think I was going to put the man in the poor house if I got a fuzzy picture of the top of his head. So, I whipped up my camera and took a picture. At that same moment, somehow, Fillion happened to not only look  up, but he saw me through the whole crowd. He pointed at me, telling me not to take photos. I apologized and felt mortified that he caught me. For a while. I don't now.

By the time I got through the line and finally met him, I don't know if he remembered my offense. Probably not since he didn't really even look up as he signed my picture. Not that he wasn't nice, he was just sort of working the assembly line, so to speak. Plus, I was paying attention to my son's conversation with Tudyk, who was very nice and seemed to think it was genuinely cool he was now a gamer tag. But I came away with a blurry picture of Fillion pointing at me angrily. I think I like that better than if it had just been him sitting there smiling.

On the Other Hand, the '*Fly* Girls Like Me

Another table was occupied by *Firefly* stars Morena Baccarin and Jewel Staite. I paid for signed photos of each. One of them was being handled by her fan club (I'm pretty sure it was Baccarin). In other words, the fan club people were taking the money and giving tickets for fans to give to her minder at the table so that person knew what we had paid for.

So, I got their autographs and even had a little chat with them. They were both very nice. But I had misunderstood what my ticket bought me. I asked if I could get a photo with Baccarin, and she said "sure" and started to stand up when her fan club minder stopped her and said I would have to go back to their ticket area and buy another ticket allowing me to get a photo with her. I apologized and said I thought I had gotten that, but apparently, I had not. Baccarin looked really embarrassed. Staite even looked a little bothered. So, I said it was cool, never mind, and Baccarin apologized to me and said it was her fan club's rules (which I interpreted as not being instated by her;

I'm assuming that money, at least some of it, went to the club). Baccarin seems to have been doing quite nicely career-wise since then and probably could not have cared less if I paid another $25 or whatever to stand next to her for half a second—which I refused to do out of principle. So Morena, you rock even if I couldn't get a photo with you.

My Almost Childhood Friend Robbie McNeill

Before my Dragon Con days, I once went to a con back when *Star Trek: Voyager* was airing and where series actor Robert Duncan McNeill was a guest. Just before the con, I happened to read an article about him which stated he was born in Georgia but spent some of his youth in Washington, D.C. Well, I grew up in D.C. and had a friend named Bobby McNeill who looked pretty much like him. RDM and I are also the same age. I started wondering if by some strange chance my Bobby and RDM were one in the same.

So, when I was getting his autograph, I brought that up. He stopped writing, put down his pen, and really chatted me up about it. He told me what school he had attended, which wasn't mine, so I knew he wasn't the kid I was thinking of. However, since we both did live there at the same time, we had a quick chat about it. In fact, the line just stopped while we talked, and I was fearing the Con Police would drag me away, so I was actually sort of making moves to continue on my way, but RDM was still talking. It did eventually get to the point where a con volunteer basically told us to stop talking and move the line along!

That's the only time I've had the celebrity have to be told to stop talking to me. So that was cool, even though he didn't turn out to be my long-lost friend.

Don't Mess with Wesley Crusher

Then there's my experience meeting Wil Wheaton (back when he was playing Wesley on *Star Trek: The Next Generation*). I was attending the con with my now-ex-husband. I was first in line to meet him, so I did my usual "thank you for coming to the convention" bit, but my husband decided to make a joke about the fact that Wheaton had probably a half dozen watches on his arm. This was a thing back in the late 80's. I think it was even better if they were all the Swatch brand. I was a huge Swatch fan myself but never did the multi-watch thing.

Anyway, my ex asked Wheaton what time it was, which was admittedly uncool for a number of reasons. But worse, Wheaton was not only very young, but he was painfully aware there was a large contingent of fans who hated his character. To be honest, I wasn't a fan of the character myself. I saw him as a misguided plot device to draw younger viewers. Having a token young person wasn't the issue; it was that Wesley did all kinds of ridiculous things, like piloting a brand-new flagship and regularly saving the day. Of course, that wasn't Wheaton's fault, and I was happy to meet him and add him to my autograph collection. So, I pretended I did not know my ex-husband as Wheaton expressed his lack of amusement. I can't remember what he said, but he definitely took offense. Part of me felt he needed to chill out, but I also knew he came into these gigs a little defensively to begin with. Sorry Wil, I didn't say it. You can wear as many watches as you like.

"I'm Neelix"

In 2000, I went to on a lunch cruise in Marina Del Rey, CA with most of the main male cast members of *Star Trek: Voyager*. It had been a long time since I had visited Los Angeles and had been wanting to go back. My son was nine and old enough to appreciate it, plus he also watched the show, so I thought it would be a cool trip for us. Technically this wasn't really a convention; it was having lunch on a boat with only about 30 other people, but I consider it a mini-con.

As we walked up to the boat entrance, the actors were waiting in a sort of receiving line to introduce themselves. They all shook hands and said something like, "Robert Beltran, nice to meet you." Obviously, they didn't really need to introduce themselves; we wouldn't be there if we didn't know who they were. But it was polite. Anyway, we got to Ethan Philips, and he reached out his hand and introduced himself as his character, Neelix. He might have done that because I had my son with me (who was the only child there) and thought he didn't understand the idea of actors and characters. Or maybe he thought he was unrecognizable out of his makeup. But then again, with a group of fans that shouldn't be an issue.

Anyway, when we got to our table, my son asked, "What's up with Ethan Phillips? Does he think he really *is* Neelix?" So, I gave him my best guess as to why he might have introduced himself that way. It wasn't a big deal at the time, but what I found amusing is my son remembered that for years after. Whenever we'd watch *Voyager* and Philips came on, my son would say "I'm Neelix." Apparently, he thought it was pretty funny. He still remembers it.

The Cigarette Smoking Man is Not to be Feared

Why? Because he may be hiding from *you*. I recently went to Spooky Empire where they had most of the cast of *The X-Files*, of which I'm a huge fan. Because I dropped a huge lump of cash to get VIP tickets and a photo with Gillian Anderson and David Duchovny together[1], I didn't buy tickets for any other celeb guest. I really did want to meet some of them, but I couldn't afford it and had to be satisfied with being in a Mulder and Scully sandwich—WORTH IT.

Anyway, while I was waiting in line for Duchovny's autograph (yeah, paid extra for that too so I could actually say something to him), there was a huge area where nobody was wandering about, and on the other side was William B. Davis's table. I figured that candid shots weren't allowed, but hey, did I mention I paid a lot of money to

---

[1] Editors' Note: The photo ops at these events are essentially a bullpen where 100s or 1000s of fans are corralled, standing, for hours to spend exactly 5 seconds posing for a photo. Conversation with the celebrities is mostly non-existent.

be at this con? I had a completely clear—albeit it rather distant—view of him. So, I held up my phone as covertly as possible and took a  picture. A con volunteer caught me and said that wasn't allowed. Unlike when I snapped a picture of Nathan Fillion, Davis didn't see me, so I didn't have to worry about the Syndicate kidnapping me for my indiscretion and turning me into an alien hybrid. It was also not a great picture.

Not to worry; I knew that the celebs I didn't spend $60 to meet would be at the VIP party, so while I might or might not get an autograph or photo with them, it would still be cool to shake their hands and say it was nice to meet them. Annabeth Gish was there and was very open to meeting people (I missed the chance, but she was staying on my hotel floor and we met in the elevator. Mind you, I didn't say anything to her; I just smiled when we made eye contact. But hey, whatever, that was cool). Another celebrity (not an *X-Files* cast member and someone I had met before) was being bitchy, so I blew her off.

But then in came Davis. He's a big part of the show and I really did want to meet him. I was with two other fans I had befriended who also hoped to meet Davis at the party, and we started over towards him. But he literally walked in the door, turned around about halfway into the room, and walked out. Apparently, the celebs were required to attend the VIP party, but how long they had to stay was up to them!

Now, I don't want to totally dis Cigarette Smoking Man: Maybe he had an attack of IBS or something like those commercials where the sufferers keep leaving parties to hit the toilet. But it looked more like he was dragging himself through an unwanted contractual obligation. I've also heard he isn't comfortable with crowds, and if that's the case, I feel for him. But still, I regretted not getting a quick handshake.

Beam Me up Scotty

As an example of what cons were like back in the day (mid-80s through maybe early 90s) when you didn't have to pay much—if anything—past the cost of admission, I managed to meet a lot of stars, many repeatedly. I've sat on James Doohan's lap more times than Santa's. And I didn't have to pay a cent for that. Of course, I'm sure Jimmy D. didn't mind having young women sitting on his lap either. RIP Scotty, you also rock.

Same goes for George Takei. I saw him so many times back then that he probably started to recognize me. And he's still awesome. Oh my!

So, there they are, a few anecdotes. There are many more, especially if I include my time working on camera, but that's another story for another book!

8 THE UNEXPECTED BEING OF STELLA
Sally L. Gage

I am going to start by saying I have always been an odd duck; one that walks the fringe and howls at the moon. For years, I never looked anyone in the eye and I always spoke in low tones so as to not draw attention to my already awkward 6-foot tall, large breasted frame, which may be an ideal in an anime cosplay but was not the norm in Manistee, Michigan, where I was laughed at and made fun of for my size. My constant companions were my animals, my movies, my television shows, and my books (probably about animals or movies or television shows) and my growing love of folklore. I hid my body and nurtured my mind. After all, growing up in rural Michigan, I had little contact with physical pop culture worlds (such as science fiction conventions). I had seen them in magazines and I had always dreamed of going to at least one so that I could experience the inclusivity I had craved. I had built up in my mind what a convention was…home.

I started going to fan conventions when I moved to Florida in the early 1990's and I quickly fell in love with everything about them. The cosplay, the parties, the comradery, and the like-minded people began to fill my blessed little geeky heart and I soon expanded my fandoms to include comic books, video games, and collectables. I released my body to fill out all those fun costumes and character dresses, and I gave my brain a vacation from all that reading. But like

many first loves, my relationship with cons began to fall apart after I was sexually assaulted going back to my room after a drunken party at a convention. I never wore my *Star Tek* uniform again. The innocent fun was no longer safe for me and I began a spiral of self-destructive behaviors that ultimately led to me gaining a metric ton of weight and developing extreme social anxiety disorder. I then stopped going to conventions altogether and went back to school. My body was once again hidden and my mind released upon the world. I became an anthropologist: a studier of people and their cultures. I also began to focus on the folklore of werewolves, always a favorite, and it led me to where I am today.

In the meantime, friends would continue to go to conventions near and far and regale us with pictures and anecdotal incidents. I would always feel a huge pang of loss and regret for not participating. The neglect of my health, my age, and an ensuing knee injury left me with a nice list of mental disorders to help cope with my new-found big brain and big body. I felt I could no longer participate in the cosplay arena or even go to a convention because "crazy fat chick" is not what I wanted to be labeled as. But stories of the openness, inclusion, and awesomeness of the east coast titan Dragon Con began to entice me. When 2013 rolled around, I was soon to be married and our gift was a honeymoon to Dragon Con, which just about coincided with the time my little bundle of joy was to arrive.

Now I know you are probably thinking I was pregnant, but alas no: I was expecting the arrival of Stella, a WerePup. I had waited for her for just over a year, and I was so excited to finally see her. You see, my love of werewolf folklore had led to an artist named Asia Eriksen and her film-quality artisan dolls called WerePups™. They were not cheap, as each one is individually made to order and thus one of a kind, and my Stella was going to be the crown jewel of my growing werewolf collection[1].

On August 23rd, she arrived. I was at work and I was told I had received a box from Pennsylvania (the WerePups' home State). I screamed and…waited not so patiently for my soon to be spouse to arrive with my boxed bundle of joy. Before the hour was out, a five-pound hairy little werewolf was being cradled in my arms and tears flowed freely. I was a WerePup Mom.

It sounds silly, I know, but this was the closest I would ever get to being a first-time mom (excluding adopting cats). Everyone who

---

[1] For more information about WerePups and Asia Eriksen, see Terry Oakes Paine's chapter in Part Three of this book.

came into my workplace that day was shocked yet fascinated by the craftmanship Asia had produced. I felt, for the first time, an overwhelming sense of pride and honor just by owning one of these creatures.

Little did I know what was to come...

Less than forty-eight hours later, car packed with suitcases, stroller, and werewolves, we were in Atlanta, Georgia for the Honeymoon at Dragon Con. I had made sure that the prescription for my anxiety medication was filled, as friends had warned me that seventy thousand people was the estimated attendance count...and my social anxiety was looking to go into full tilt overload. Not to mention our hotel would probably look sideways at us for having a werewolf being toted about the place.

We were wholly unprepared for the reality of Dragon Con as we checked into our hotel (not a host hotel, but a rather pricey one nearby). "Luxurious" is a word I would use to describe the place; glass shimmered in the sunlight and the cool, wide-open spaces of the lobby made us feel welcome, though a bit out of place. We were more used to the Motel 6 accommodations than this fancy Atlanta hotel, but we needed to sit and be calm to gather our thoughts after the long drive from Florida. We knew we would need to go down and get our badges eventually, but for that moment, we just sat, taking it all in. Imagine our surprise when a beautiful musical artist named Brandy flounced by and more limousines pulled up outside. Yea, this place wasn't just fancy...it was opulent.

I kept Stella kind of hidden from view as we got settled into our room and planned out where to go and get our badges, where to eat, and what to see. But we wanted to get started, so we went down to the site and realized badges were being given out separately to the pre-purchasers (which we were), so we jumped in line. It wasn't so bad—the line only wrapped halfway around the hotel and the wait was only a few hours—but then the subtly deceptive heat of August in Atlanta began to take shape.

I figured while we waited in line I could bring Stella out of her hiding bag and test the waters. She was so wonderfully received and it made the sweltering wait more bearable. People asked questions and, startled, I mumbled through answers the best I could. They held her, took pictures, and snapped selfies with this truly unique doll. We continued standing in the sun, moving forward little by little, step by step, sharing Stella with people as they passed us to get in the back of the ever-growing queue.

By the time we reached the front of the line…I passed out, thus breaking in the first aid response team *and* first aid room for Dragon Con 2013.

By the time we returned to the hotel room, hours later, we knew medication was in order for the days to follow, and the next morning, I carefully swallowed my pills with orange juice and a banana. I was drugged, chilled, and chilling in the air-conditioned hall while we waited for our picture with the *Torchwood* cast.

And as we sat waiting for the photo op to begin, a very handsome, leather clad actor came running at me, arms extended in grabby-hands position, squealing "werewolf, werewolf, werewolf!" I have to admit, I was not only chilled by the Xanax, but also too distracted by his rippling pectorals and lace-up, form-fitting leather pants to realize that it was Manu Bennett, an actor from New Zealand who is as beautiful in person as he is on film.

Bennett swooped in, scooped up Stella...and proceeded to bounce and cradle her—then ran about the room with other folks in tow. It took a moment before I truly realized that he had run off with my very expensive doll! Just then, he reappeared with Stella, and stopped to talk with a few other people, before returning the WerePup to my waiting arms. Stella had survived her first celebrity mauling—and it was certainly not her last. I will never forget him for the rest of my life.

We continued on what was to be our first scheduled photo op of the weekend. The *Torchwood* cast members responded in varying degrees of shock and fascination. I had never heard John Barrowman scream before that moment and I thought Eve Myles was going to pass out when she saw Stella and Silas, our latex toddler werewolf. We discovered later that Eve Myles was three months pregnant at the

time; which probably explains the freaked out look on her face in the photo.

Over four days of the convention, we met multiple celebrities, ran into old friends, and made new friends. We ate new foods and discovered that just sitting in the lobby of the Marriot with a stroller full of werewolves was enough to draw crowds to us. Famous people stopped to take selfies. Cosplayers acted out scenes from various televisions shows and movies, using Stella as a prop. Guests stopped cold and ran over to us, asking "what IS that? Can I hold it?" I found it useful to create a  "script" explaining who Stella was, that I was not the artist who made her, and that yes, it was okay to take her photo and pose with her. We took so many photos that we ended up deleting cat pictures to make room for WerePup encounters.

The people, the costumes, and celebrities were a blur of activity and experiences, but like everything, the convention had to come to an end. We returned to the hotel, packed our bags, and started filling the car with suitcases and souvenirs. As we came down the elevator for the last time, Jonathon, our consigliere, ran up and hugged us. Several staff members came out to hold Stella one final time. Tears flowed, and we saw that the hotel had given us a 15% "werewolf discount" off our bill and I felt I was leaving home.

It during our drive home, as we talked and laughed, that I realized I had not taken any of my medication for anxiety since the first day. We pondered the implications and wondered if this was a fluke or if it actually could have been the presence of a silicone werewolf that acted as a placebo in place of the medications.

We geared up, not that long after Dragon Con, to go to a small local convention, Necronomicon, and we got a booth to sell our jewelry and put our theory regarding the WerePup Placebo to the test. Necronomicon is nowhere near the size of Dragon Con, but it is well-attended for a local event and good for the initial trial of the theory. I was nervous at first, but I figured that since the event was so close to home, that if something went wrong, I would be okay. I perched behind our table, and propped Stella up to take in the view. We were in front of the home-built TARDIS someone had provided for photos, and more than one cosplayer asked to pose holding Stella. After a while, I realized I was not nervous at all!

Although I do not recommend doing this without medical supervision, I went and participated in the whole event without the need for meds…only Stella. It was a dream. People were open and curious, and I answered all of their questions without hesitation. I had no panic attacks, no black outs: only warm memories and a familiar feeling of home returning.

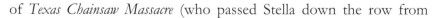

The next week, we visited Spooky Empire, a horror convention in Orlando. Guests included the late great George Romero, who eagerly agreed to hold Stella for our photo and the cast of *Texas Chainsaw Massacre* (who passed Stella down the row from person to person). Once, again, I tested the WerePup Placebo Theory, and realized to my delight, that this was not a fluke. I could attend small and large conventions without needing my medication!

What I also realized was that, with Stella, my love for conventions returned full tilt. In the past, my body size and body dysmorphia, combined with social anxiety disorder, had made it difficult, if not impossible, to participate in one of my favorite pastimes. With Stella, I could be seen not just as a WerePup Mom Cosplayer (which is what people usually assume), but also as a creative person. The focus is not on me, but on my WerePup, and I find it easy—not to mention fun—to interact with celebrities and convention-goers alike. Thanks to a little silicone werewolf, I can once again rejoin my convention-going family. Not only that, but since 2013, I have started attending conventions as a Guest Author, appearing on various panels (with  Stella, of course). I find it easy to talk to others as long as I have her with me. I don't know how to explain why she works so well, but I am grateful every day for her presence, and for the acceptance I feel from others because of her.

PART THREE
EXCELLENT ECLECTIC
ADVENTURES

9 A VERY MEGA CONVENTION EXPERIENCE
Dee Fish[2]

In 2017, I was a guest at the Orlando MegaCon comics and pop culture expo in Florida. I had lived in Florida for over twenty years prior, but this would be my first Orlando show since moving to Pennsylvania in 2015. MegaCon in Orlando was the first convention I had ever been to as a comic creator and not just a fan, starting in 2002 after launching my then-ongoing WebComic, *Dandy and Company*. And, except for the 2016 show, I had been back every year since.

But that year would be different for another reason. It would also be my first Orlando MegaCon since coming out as Transgender. This time, I would be there as "Dee Fish", not…that other guy.

I was going to be there promoting the successful Kickstarter for a comic book collecting my then-new Webcomic. The Webcomic, *Finding Dee,* chronicled the trials and tribulations of coming out as trans in your 40s while still trying to make it as a successful artist and writer in comics. I would have printed copies of the first issue and was looking forward to reconnecting with friends and industry

---

[2] All original art in this chapter created by Dee Fish, who has graciously permitted us to use her wonderful work. For more information go to: https://www.patreon.com/bigpondcomics

professionals I'd not seen since leaving Florida. Well, the ones that still talked to me. There were a small handful of folks that essentially pretended I'd never existed and I was happy to return the favor.

As my girlfriend and I made our way on the 20+ hour drive from Pennsylvania to Florida, there was one aspect of the trip that I'd forgotten to research: Did they have single-occupancy restrooms in the Orlando Convention Center? In the two years since I had come out, this kind of research had become almost like second nature to me. Single-occupancy restrooms were legally safe to use and as a transgender woman, I had become accustomed to finding out in advance where I would be able to go pee without being challenged on it when I went places. As we discovered on the day of the show, there were no such facilities in the building we were in.

Like many transgender women, I am utterly terrified about going to the bathroom in public spaces. The media circus stirred up with North Carolina's horrifying laws—which wanted to make it a criminal act for me, as a woman, to use public women's restrooms based on utter fear-mongering and nothing more—had permeated the national conversation and was made worse by becoming a talking point for the GOP during the 2016 elections. See, my driver's license says "female," but thanks to political scapegoating, many states now have laws that mean that if I go into a women's restroom, I've just committed a crime and can be arrested. Of course, there are virtually no cases of transgender women ever doing anything inappropriate in public restrooms.

However, the laundry list of physical assaults, rapes, and worse that occur every year when draconian laws force transgender women into men's rooms grows longer every year. Unbridled, and meaningless, fear had made it a very real danger for trans people just trying to navigate the world. Use the room that is correct for who and what I am and face jail time and a criminal record. Use the room conservatives tell me I should, and get the shit kicked out of me or worse. Heck, even single occupancy restrooms aren't always incident free. A local Karaoke bar we frequent has a locking, single occupancy ladies' room and I was yelled at by a drunk woman for using it and then she went and complained to the owner.

So, by the time MegaCon had come, I had already accumulated a moderate list of negative bathroom experiences: Other customers at bars and restaurants complaining to the management being the most common and I was terrified by the possibility of having to hold my bladder for a three-day convention. The Friday of the show went okay. Being a guest gave me access to restrooms cut off from the rest of the crowd behind the scenes which was still stressful, but more manageable and everything went well. Saturday, however, was a different story.

That same Friday at a Convention in another state, there was apparently a gunman that had been apprehended trying to enter the con floor and as a result, MegaCon's security was increased significantly. I didn't know the reason at the time, though. All I knew was that at EVERY bathroom in the convention center, there was a security guard sitting in a chair at the door. My heart sank and I went numb.

In my paranoid mind, somebody MUST have complained about the 6'2" "tranny" using the bathrooms the day before. I began to panic. I began making calls to friends who were on the show management to find out what was going on and to find out if there was ANYwhere I could go without worrying. By the middle of the day, I didn't have any answers. What I DID have was a Panel that I was scheduled to present on called "LGBTQ+ Representation in Comics." And boy, did I have to pee!

Making my way across the convention center, passing guarded bathroom after guarded bathroom, I was getting increasingly nervous. I was set to be on the panel with the industry who's who of professionals that were also representative of the LGBTQ+ community. It was supposed to be Marc Andreyko, Cat Staggs, Amanda Deibert, Phil Jimenez, Tara Ford, Tee Franklin, Jose Villarubia, and me. The main topic to be discussed was the *LOVE IS LOVE* book put together to benefit the families of the victims of the Pulse Nightclub massacre. To give you an idea of how out of my league I felt, the convention program book listed everyone else on the panel only by their last names, except for me. I was the only attendee not well known enough to merit simply being "Fish." This was something that had happened on panels even before I changed my name, but it was always a not-so-subtle reminder of my lack of overall notoriety in the industry. And it was a taste of what was to come.

When I showed up at the door, I came across a half full audience and a completely empty stage. Chairs, a table, and microphones, but no other guests. I talked to the convention volunteer working the door and they didn't know where anyone was even though the panel was about to begin. After a little bit, I learned that the premier of *Wonder Woman* was happening in Hollywood and half the panelists had been invited, so they skipped the con that day. The rest were actually informed by the con staff that the panel had been rescheduled until the next day. The lady who wasn't important enough to be just a last name had *not* been informed. Neither had the audience.

So, with massive nerves, I stepped up onto the stage by myself, facing an awaiting room and a thumbs up to just go from the volunteer. I sat there for a few silent moments staring at the crowd nervously before one of my more bizarre superpowers kicked in.

So, first some context. I have massive social anxiety. If you meet me just walking around somewhere, I will not know how to talk to you. I get clammy and anxious and forget how to talk to humans. But if you give me a MICROPHONE, I somehow transform into a low-rent stand-up comedian and rock star. I immediately grabbed that mic and started singing "Don't Stop Believing" by Journey.

After my impromptu performance, I began making some jokes and talking to the crowd, doing my best to explain that nobody else was apparently coming. Soon, I began fielding questions. Folks started asking about the charity book and I had to inform them that I was the only LGBTQ creator scheduled to be on the panel who was not included in the book. A small item of note: nobody knew who I am. ☺

Book One: For the Love of the Con

So, then there were a lot of the questions you would expect and the homophobic comments phrased as questions like:

- "Why did they have to make LaFou gay in the new *Beauty and the Beast*?"
- "Why not just create a new character instead of making hero-X gay?"
- "I'm fine with that so long as they don't shove it down our throats!"

And my personal favorite:

- "Why does sexuality have to come into stories at all? Just tell a good story, I don't care who's fucking who?"

That's a chestnut that ignores that HETEROsexuality is a staple of almost every story you've ever read or seen. Don't believe me? *Star Wars* was billed with the tagline, "The Story of a Boy, a Girl, and a Galaxy!"

Are you a fan of *Harry Potter*? Then you've probably heard people complain about Dumbledore being gay with clichés like: "It's a story about wizards! Nobody cares about their sexuality!" This, of course, ignores the nearly endless list of HEREROsexual relationships and couples in the series that, by that logic, should not have been mentioned. Harry and Ginny, Harry and Cho, Cho and Cedric, Hermione and Ron, Hermione and Viktor, Lily and James, Lily and Snape, and so on and so forth.

Let's think of some other famous stories that have heterosexuality thrown into them in ways that those complaints choose to ignore: *The Matrix, The Incredibles, Star Trek, Lord of the Rings, The X-Men, Spider-Man*...heck, EVERY Superhero movie up until, I think, *Captain Marvel*. The point being is that when heterosexuality is "shoved down our throats," it's perfectly acceptable to the same people that feel personally attacked at even the HINT of a homosexual attraction. Amazingly, it seems that sexuality is only acceptable when it's the same as the person making that inane complaint. But I digress.

Anyway, after answering those questions, the topic turned towards what kinds of hurdles to LGBTQ+ creators have to face in comics. For my part, I decided to make a little point and I mentioned that for me, as the "T" in "LGBTQ+," the problems were the ones I faced everywhere: You are misgendered, deadnamed, and treated like a default-sexual predator. Deadnamed, if you are unfamiliar with the term, is when somebody uses the name you went by prior to coming out, either by accident or with malicious intent. You have former industry friends accuse you of "faking it for publicity and attention," and you have former fans write you emails to inform you that they will be tearing up all of the art they commissioned from you because your happiness has disappointed them so.

And at some conventions, you couldn't use the bathroom with impunity.

Sure, I COULD use the bathroom. But I could also risk being verbally harassed by those security guards for trying to walk in to the women's restroom. And, as I said before, using the men's room often leads to assault and worse. I've been extremely fortunate to have avoided such attacks so far, but countless other transgender individuals are not so lucky and the stories of beatings, rapes, hospitalizations, and deaths would turn your stomach. I could be accused of committing a crime by someone in there or beaten by the angry boyfriends outside. And I was an INVITED guest.

As I finished the panel, I shared the stories of my day of not peeing and desperately needing to.

Then something very unexpected happened: A young woman in the crowd raised her hand. As I answered to see if she had a question, she simply said "If you want, you can come with me."

Seconds later, the woman next to her nodded and added her name to that statement. Within a few seconds, I had nearly a dozen women agreeing to create a veritable "pee gang" to escort me to the bathroom and give anyone who had anything to say about it hell. It was everything I could do not to cry right there on the stage.

So, as the panel ended, a few folks in the audience had some questions, and some wanted to know where my table was. But that group of women were standing there waiting and we all went pee together.

Well, not "together" together, but you get my point. ☺

The next day, the real panel happened and I was on it for real and pretty much nobody cared who I was. But for one brief hour, I had a girl-posse and that was kind of amazing. In reality, it turned out to be one of the most positive memories that I often cling to when the world shows its ugly side.

I still have to deal with all these same problems. Gotta pee after a movie? Better hope it's not busy in the theater. Most restaurants don't have single occupancy restrooms where I live, so actually being able to use the restroom before or after a meal usually involves going somewhere safe before or holding it until I get home.

But I thought conventions would be better and so far, they really have been about the same as anywhere else: Dirty looks and disgusted parents clutching their children away from me. And I still haven't been back to Heroes Con in North Carolina in spite of the wonderful showrunner, Shelton Drum, assuring me personally that he would make sure it was safe. Eisner Award winning colorist Laura Martin told me that if I came back, she would arrange a similar posse of female creators to escort me to the bathrooms of the Charlotte Convention Center. But I'm still scared. Laws of the state trump the best intentions of wonderful people.

But it's those wonderful people that keep me coming back to conventions. The peers who have told me that they would stand with me and make sure it was safe. Or that local bar owner who, at the end, told that drunk woman to take her business elsewhere in my defense.

So not every story ends badly. And sometimes people will surprise you. And I'll always cherish that day when a group of women dressed as the superheroes they really were created a human shield of compassion so I could pee in peace.

CONVENTIONALLY SPEAKING

Book One: For the Love of the Con

10 "I'M JUST HERE FOR THE BACKSTREET BOYS"
Mara Sansolo

Setting the Scene

When you think of a Walker Stalker convention, you probably envision actors from *The Walking Dead*, or other zombie characters. What you likely don't think of is the Backstreet Boys.

Yes, I went to two zombie conventions just to see a Backstreet Boy.

Let me say up front, I do not like zombies, and *The Walking Dead* freaks me out: I couldn't get past the first episode. However, I would do just about anything for a Backstreet Boy; which led me to attend Walker Stalker in Atlanta in 2016 and 2017.

The story starts with an obscure SyFy movie called *Dead 7*, which was written by Backstreet Boy Nick Carter (the blonde one), and starred members of other boybands such as NSYNC, 98 Degrees, and O-Town. Nick raised funds on Indiegogo for his "boyband zombie movie," and SyFy aired it for the first time in early 2016. It was the quintessential SyFy movie: so horrible, that you couldn't help but watch the whole thing. If there had not been a Backstreet Boy involved, I never would have watched it.

So, let me give you some background on my history with BSB. I have been a fan since 1997, have attended over thirty concerts, and I have gone on five cruises with them. The cruises are kind of like a little fan convention themselves, since you are stuck on a boat for a week with 2,000 other girls who are just as crazy as you are, and as a bonus, you run into the Boys all over the ship, and there are nightly parties and concerts. My travels to see BSB include much of the eastern seaboard of the US, along with Las Vegas, and yes, I have traveled to Europe to see them.

Like most fan groups, BSB fandom is a pretty tight-knit group, and through my travels and social media, I have met some of the people whom I consider to be my best friends, including one who lives about an hour from me, and three who live in the Atlanta area. This is the core group of us that went to Walker Stalker Atlanta in 2016 and 2017. My friends were all either familiar with *The Walking Dead*, or knew some of the actors from other projects they had worked on, but I walked in to the convention to see one person, and one person only. My favorite Backstreet Boy, Nick Carter.

2016

In August 2016, Walker Stalker announced that Nick Carter would be making an appearance at the Atlanta convention in October, and since Atlanta was as close as he was going to get to Florida for a while, my friends and I decided to make a weekend of it. As soon as they announced Nick's appearance, I coordinated with my "team" and booked a flight to Atlanta and a hotel for the weekend. I had no idea what to expect at Walker Stalker, especially since I don't typically like things that are scary, but I knew it would be worth it.

Flash forward to two days before the convention. I was in an important meeting at work, when my smartwatch suddenly went crazy with alerts, messages, and tweets from friends. Turns out, Nick had some sort of emergency and would be unable to attend the convention. At this point, the hotel and flights were already paid for, as was my pass for the convention, so there was no going back, unless I wanted to lose a chunk of money. Once I got over the shock of him canceling, I decided that this could just be a fun girls' weekend, anyway; one where I would get to see friends that I would only otherwise get to see once or twice a year.

I flew up on Friday, and, upon arrival in Atlanta, we all met up and decided that since we had paid for passes to the convention, we would at least attend for a few hours on Saturday. As I mentioned earlier, I had no interest in anyone else at the convention, but I was fine to hang out with my friends while they got selfies with assorted actors. I mostly wandered around, and to my surprise, there were a lot of families at the convention, which makes a deal of billing itself as family friendly. That would not have been my first thought when someone brings up a zombie event, but there was not anything that was overtly scary out in the main area. I believe they had a walk-through set up with zombie scenes, and that was frightening to me, but the general atmosphere of the conference was not terrifying at all. There were a lot of merchandise vendors, and I ended up purchasing a lanyard that had pugs on it (at a zombie convention).

There was one booth that I was drawn to from the moment that we walked in to the convention center. There was a tattoo area set up, with about ten artists from all around the country. At this point in

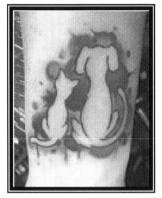

my life, I had two tattoos, both of which could be completely covered by regular clothing, but I had also started working for a company that was a lot more casual than my previous employers, and plenty of people had visible tattoos there. I think my hair was purple at the time, as well. I took the plunge, and on the spot, decided that I wanted a tattoo on my wrist.

The tattoo took about an hour, which brought us to lunch time. After we ate, some of the others still had a few celebrities they wanted to meet, so I hung out in the convention hall for a while longer. We really did not stay long and left early for a nice dinner at the Hard Rock Café. Because the flight and hotel were already booked and paid for well before Nick canceled, I still got to have one more free day in Atlanta.

The next day, we did the "Atlanta tourist thing" and went to the World of Coca-Cola and the Olympic Centennial Park. I joke that I may not have gotten a photo with Nick Carter that weekend, but I did get a picture with the Coca-Cola polar bear mascot. By the time we had sampled sodas from around the world, it was time to head back to the airport, because I had to be back at work the next morning. All in all, it was an enjoyable weekend with friends, but it sure would have been nicer if there had been a Backstreet Boy there, as well.

2017

2017 was vastly different from 2016, since there were no cancellations. In fact, the Backstreet Boys even performed as a group at a radio station concert on Friday night, so everyone was in town. This time, I drove the eight hours up to Atlanta, rather than fly. The convention was Friday through Sunday, and Nick was going to be there on Friday and Saturday.

By the time I got into town on Friday afternoon, my first thought was to go directly to the concert. But then about two hours prior to the start, Nick tweeted that he was at the convention. The perk of this radio station concert was that BSB were the headliners, and therefore would not start their set until 10pm, so my other friend (who had driven up from Orlando) and I got in the car and drove from the hotel to the convention center, hoping to get a glimpse of Nick before he left for the concert. We got to the convention center around 5:30pm, and quickly got in line to take a picture with him. In addition to getting a few selfies, Nick was kind enough to record an outgoing message for my voicemail. So, if by chance, you ever call me, and I do not answer, you will get a message from a Backstreet Boy.

We sped through the line, and then got back on the road to head to Alpharetta for the concert, which was about a 40-minute drive (plus Atlanta traffic). There were 4-5 acts at the radio station concert, and we missed the first two, but made it in time for the big names. Luckily, my friend and I had purchased seats up close, rather than being in the General Admission pit area. To be frankly honest, I did not care for the other acts, but BSB performed about half of what they sing nightly at their Las Vegas residency, so my night was made.

Saturday was the main day of the convention, with a whole group of us attending. After I had gotten that "of the moment" tattoo the previous year, I decided to make it a tradition. However, this time I was prepared and had a design and an appointment with a tattoo artist all set up. The last time I went to a zombie convention, I got a dog and cat tattoo. This time, at the zombie convention, I got a much larger Winnie the Pooh tattoo. I had the first tattoo appointment of the morning, so they let me into the convention center early, and it took about two hours. While the tattoos I  got at Walker Stalker were in no way related to the Backstreet Boys, I should note that I have two BSB tattoos in my ever-growing collection.

By the time my tattoo was finished, all of my friends started arriving at the convention, and Nick was scheduled to be there all day for selfies, panels, and official photo ops. Each celebrity who was at Walker Stalker had a line that you could go through to get an autograph, a selfie, or just talk to the person. Even though I had gone through Nick's line and spoken to him the night before, we all queued up to see him again on Saturday. This time the selfies were silly, since I have plenty of serious pictures with him already. When I told one of my friends that he had recorded my voicemail greeting, she had him do the same for her, so we both have very unique voicemail recordings!

Early in the afternoon Nick did a panel. I honestly do not remember what it was about, but I am sure it had to do with *Dead 7*.

Some of my friends got up front for the panel, but I hung out in the back, just taking everything in. After the panel, it was time for the official convention photo op with the professional photographer (versus my iPhone). Nick admittedly had one of the shorter lines for a photo op, and it was a very quick process. Pose, smile, next! I much rather prefer the interaction at the tables, but I wanted to have a professional photo in addition to my silly selfies.

BSB Forever?

Unfortunately, no Backstreet Boys made an appearance at Walker Stalker 2018, but that was fine with me. One of my friends from Atlanta ended up winning a radio station contest for a free trip to see BSB in Las Vegas that same weekend, and I got to go with her to that. We had a free flight, hotel, and tickets to the show. I may not have been at a zombie convention, but the last weekend in October usually seems to revolve around the Backstreet Boys now! Even though I had no interest in the zombie part of the convention, I have to say, everyone I encountered at Walker Stalker was insanely nice. In 2016, we had shirts made that said, "I'm Only Here for Nick Carter," and all of the Walker Stalker staff thought they were hysterical, especially since we wore them even after we knew he was not going to be there.

I don't foresee myself ever going to another Walker Stalker unless there is a Backstreet Boy involved, because try as I might over the years, I just cannot get into the whole zombie thing. It freaks me out. But if Nick Carter were to ever make another appearance at a convention on the east coast of the United States, you know I will be there. I may not have gotten to see Nick in both years, but I still have something to show from those two weekends, which are two of my favorite tattoos (I am now up to fifteen and counting).

11 STAR(K) TREK
Brandy Stark

I was a nerdy child. This was already a challenge during my childhood years, but my attendance at an all-girl's Catholic school created even greater difficulties. I was a student of this place from middle school through high school, where I graduated in a class of 60 students. In such a limited population, I was a true social minority. I found little to bond over with my classmates: I didn't like clothes shopping, was not excessively wealthy, did not have deep family ties in the area, and I was not Catholic. Instead, I spent my time in worlds of science fiction. I secretly read comic books, and behind closed doors, I watched action cartoons like *G.I. Joe, Thundercats,* and *Transformers.* However, the thing that kept me going through all of those lonely years was my publically professed deep and abiding love for the classic *Star Trek* series.

I am not sure what first appealed to me about *Star Trek.* Perhaps early on I associated it with my parents. As the only child of a divorced couple, I often saw my parents as true opposites. They were friends even after the divorce, but my father was an introverted Republican cat-loving civil engineer employed by the government, and my mother was an extroverted Democratic dog person who worked in Human Resources through the private sector. Many days, I marvel that I exist at all from this odd couple.

The overlap emerges from a childhood memory. I know that I was about 9 years old when my mother took me to the theater to see *Star Trek III: the Search for Spock*. I did not understand why we went to

the film: My mother's tastes ranged to mysteries, and we rarely went out to see movies. She explained that the movie was from a TV show that my father liked. That added to the mysterious allure of what we were watching. At the time, though, the only impression left upon me was sadness. With no background in *Star Trek*, I did not understand the complexities of the Klingon-Kirk relationship. I knew that the Klingon Commander, Kruge, was the bad guy, but I still felt sorry for him when his pet died...even if the creature was a cross of canine and crocodile; mean and ugly.

I am not sure how I rediscovered *Star Trek*. I know that I was in middle school and had just entered into my all girl's Catholic school experience. We had just moved back to the Tampa Bay area after a couple of miserable years in South Florida where both my mother and I felt out of place. We had a townhouse in North Tampa, but it was a fair distance from the school. My mother worked full time and I had no one in close proximity to my home to play with. As a bit of a latchkey kid, my best friend was my guinea pig, Precious. This got me in trouble at the parent-teacher conferences. My teacher complained to my mother that I talked too much about the guinea pig and did not smile enough. Mom, who thought that the complaint was ridiculous, offered me 25¢ a day to smile at the woman.

This time period helped to develop my sense of independence. I spent a few hours a day alone. I worked on homework, and then watched the late afternoon cartoons that showed on WTOG 44. After *GI Joe, Transformers,* and *Thundercats* aired, the re-runs of *Star Trek* began. I often left the television on to have a bit of noise in the house and over time, I realized that this show offered several comforting ideas. This was a brave crew of intrepid men and women who explored space. They had wonderful adventures. They had friendships and strong inter-personal bonds. And, of course, they had Captain James T. Kirk.

Captain Kirk was my first television crush. He was a leader, he was intelligent, and he was fearless. I was so enamored with him that I started to create what I later learned were "Mary Sue" stories in which I inserted myself as a "Second Officer" with the same rank as Scotty but in line for leadership after Spock. I found that I could include myself with this cast of characters pretty easily and this fascinated me. I could not be bored exploring space with a group of diverse and powerful individuals.

My interest in the fandom grew as I learned of the *Star Trek* novels. When I went to visit my father in the summers, I was thrilled that he had cable since he got *Nickelodeon.* It was the only channel at the time that aired reruns of the *Star Trek: The Animated Series.* It became my father's tradition to get me the yearly *Trek* calendars; each month highlighting a different character and a different episode.

It was also during this time that I learned of the *Star Trek* conventions. I believe that my father took me to my first one. These were small fan-driven events whose guest list usually included two or three support characters and one actor from the main seven-core group. I do not remember the name of the first convention we attended, but I recall that it was moderately attended, held in a hotel, and it was an area that was bright and airy. I also remember spending time making special *Star Trek* t-shirts with puffy pen ink. I wrote "*Star Trek*" all over the shirts, then added dots and smudges to represent galaxies and stars. It took a long time for me to make each one, but all of that work paid off. Mark Leonard and Majel Barrett Roddenberry both complimented my work when I went through the line to get their autographs. It was a thrilling day for me.

This led to other conventions where I met the novelists who wrote books in the *Star Trek* universe. I specifically remember getting an autograph from the author of *The Klingon Dictionary,* Marc Okrand, as he had sparkling intelligent eyes and was quite proud of his work. Everyone was kind and inclusive. It's no wonder these events became a mainstay for me.

The pinnacle of my childhood experience came with my first encounter with William Shatner. He was the star attraction for the largest *Star Trek* convention in the United States, held in California. It was my first trip to the West Coast. My father took me and, as I was 14 at the time, I got to have my own hotel room. I remember that I was thrilled to have control over the room thermostat. The convention was larger than the others were, and it was more crowded. I remember seeing a number of the cast, but only a few stood out for me. One was Gene Rodenberry, who was a large man, but so soft spoken. I remember sitting in the audience and feeling annoyed with people who got up and left as he was talking. It showed little respect for the creator of the franchise.

When Shatner finally took the stage, I remember that I was a little disappointed. This was shortly after his *T.J. Hooker* days and the curly hair was not a favorite look for me. His presentation was also somehow so smug. His tone was one that seemed to be mocking the fans a little. Unlike Gene Rodenberry, who seemed so modest and shy, Shatner appeared to thrive on the attention. He dismissed some of the questions that fans asked about show minutia. He seemed to indicate that we were wasting his time with these questions. My feelings for Kirk dimmed a little based on this, yet, the entire event was an experience with my father that I will never forget. It was a pinnacle for me to be among so many fans and to see the people who made *Star Trek* a reality.

There was only one thing that could ruin *Star Trek* for me: the revival of the franchise with *Star Trek: The Next Generation*. I watched the first few episodes and immediately knew that I was not going to be a fan. But still, it had opened a door: the "normal" people around me suddenly discovered the franchise. It became popular. *Star Trek* was no longer my own personal paradise. It was becoming more common as a part of mainstream media. Moreover, I was rather insulted with Captain Picard as a replacement for Captain Kirk. To me, he did not hold the same adventurous nature as his predecessor, and I did not think William Riker was enough to bridge the gap. For a time, my interest in the franchise waned. It had done the one thing that I dreaded: it had mainstreamed.

With the "normies" invading my precious *Star Trek,* I moved my interest into comic books. By now, the comic market was reviving. Trading cards, action figures, and collector cover editions made the genre accessible. I started picking up issues of the *X-Men* at Woolworth's in the mall. Later, I transitioned to the local comic shop as my interests expanded to include *Legionnaires* and *Legion of Superheroes* in the DC universe. These were more marvelous tales of heroes clad in costumes that I could identify with. I had discovered my love for mythology by this time and the two genres fit together well. My mind could track powers, philosophies, and adventures easily. Thus, I found myself spending free time reading comics in my room while listening to Peter Gabriel and Sting.

I strayed from conventions for a few years until I overheard the comics crowd began to speak reverently of Dragon Con in Atlanta. This stuck with me as I moved into my undergraduate education and a job at the University of South Florida St. Petersburg library. I worked in the Technical Services department with other women who were also into science fiction fandom. Though all were older than I was, we still bonded over the ideas of *Highlander, Star Trek,* and good vampire lore like Anne Rice's *Queen of the Damned.* I learned that libraries were not always the stuffy places that they are painted to be:

it was here that I also discovered Slash fiction (which originated with the Kirk/Spock fanfic set), fanfiction groups, and e-zines. These wonderfully zany ladies had also heard of Dragon Con. A trio of us decided to go and check it out; and for many subsequent years, I—along with my science fiction-loving and self-proclaimed "Aunties"—returned for more fun.

Dragon Con of the mid-1990s was a fantastic thing. It was a large convention with a diverse group of people. It was well known among the fans but had not yet mainstreamed. I discovered that Dragon Con had a fantasy/science fiction-themed art show. As a newly budding artist myself, I decided to enter. One of my early works, depicting a sleeping baby dragon, won an award for Best 3-D. I was astounded: it was my first convention art show and my first official art award.

I continued to work with the art show for 3 years. The art show director, a fellow by the name of Patrick Roberts, ran the event. It had grown over the years and moved from the outskirts of the convention to its heart. I proposed the creation of the Dragon Con Salon, an art tour that included a handful of artists who would stand by their displays and talk to those in attendance. It was a way to get patrons to move through the area, take a closer look at the art, and get to know the artists. I spoke about religion as a source for science fiction concepts (such things as the role of the Jewish golem as inspiring both Frankenstein's monster and Superman).

Eventually, I gave up on Dragon Con and other large conventions and I stuck with Necronomicon in Tampa, a 40-year-old locally grown con that puts heart above wallet. Founded by Stone Hill SF Association, it is a labor of love created by intrepid volunteers each October. Proceeds from the convention go to help "Tampa Bay Kids and Canines," so this fact alone elevates it to the rank of superstar in my eyes. Focused on Sci-Fi/fantasy/horror literature, the convention hosts local writers, artists, and professors as speakers. A dedicated fan base comes each year. The convention is old enough that it is now multi-generational. It has become a family tradition for some. This makes it all the more fascinating for me.

For a time, though, I thought that my affair with conventions was over, but it has re-bloomed as I enter middle age. The *Star Trek* movie reboot brought me back to that fandom. I rediscovered channels that ran the original show, along with *The Next Generation, Deep Space 9, Voyager,* and *Enterprise*. The overzealous mainstreaming of *Star Trek* had largely subsided and shifted instead towards the *Star Wars* franchise. I could love the series again—and revisit the other spin off shows that were, it turned out, written with much better scripts than I recalled in my youth. The 50th anniversary of the original series was also on the horizon. And I was drawn back to the newer, larger conventions that had taken over the field. They reminded me of the old Dragon Con of the 1990s, though more organized and costlier.

In the intervening years, the crowds had changed a bit—the costumes were more professional, the dealer's room had tripled in size, and autographs were ridiculously expensive. Still, I felt a bit more at home with these people…I realized that I missed the convention scene. It was like becoming reacquainted with a friend that hadn't been around for a number of years. I even went to offbeat conventions like *Fan Boy* where I posed with Michelangelo of the *Teenaged Mutant Ninja Turtle* movies and saw Adam West and Burt Ward reunited for one of their last showings together.

In 2012, my father, the man who helped stoke my interest in the series, passed away. Perhaps nostalgia—trying to return to the memories of my youth—brought me even further back into science fiction. I drifted more into *Star Trek*.

To my surprise, a small Trek convention, *Away Mission,* popped up in 2014. Though the Tampa-based convention lasted only for a single year, this peaked my interest as it hosted William Shatner as the guest. Leonard Nimoy, who was, at the time in failing health, utilized Skype to do a video presentation for the fans. And for the first time in my life, my mother wanted to come to the convention, too. In her own way, I think she was also trying to connect with the memory of my father and perhaps to understand the rather eccentric nature of her daughter. I was glad for the company and took her to her first Sci-Fi convention when she was 71 years old.

We saw several guests speak, but the biggest draw was the autograph session with William Shatner. This time, Shatner was absolutely charming. Perhaps time had mellowed him, or he realized his place as a pop culture icon and embraced it. Either way, he won my heart back with his zest for life and advice for fans to embrace various experiences. It was more meaningful for me at the autograph table. Years ago, I had given my father a black and white photograph of the original cast. After his death, the photo was returned to me. I had the photograph specially framed with archival mat and glass. However, the frame was further specialized to allow the photograph to be removed, signed, and replaced.

Frame in hand, I marched to the autograph line. I was out of practice and the procedure had changed. The cost was $80 cash and the wait was long. The assistant took the cash and pulled out a sticky note: "Who should he sign this to? Where?" I answered the questions and the note was applied to the photograph. We moved forward. With such a streamlined process, I did not expect to have time to interact with Mr. Shatner. To my surprise, we had a brief conversation.

"I saw you when I was 14. I went to see you in California with my father. This photograph that you are signing was his. He died in 2012. But now, I have brought my mother with me to see you."

"Where is she?"

"Oh, she's here" (and I pointed to where I had last seen my mother. She had shifted to my other side so as to not get in the way, and she looked shocked when I turned to find her).

Shatner looked at her for a moment and very cordially said, "It's nice to meet you."

He then signed my piece and out we walked. For such a short conversation, I found myself on cloud 9. Mom was in shock that he spoke to her. For me, it symbolized a tie that bound my family together. Now, as an adult child of divorced parents, there was a common thread: William Shatner. *Star Trek*. Conventions.

We were both so enamored that for the next few years, Mom and I attended a smattering of conventions including MegaCon in Orlando, where we met George Takei. He, too, signed my photograph. We went to Tampa Bay Comic Con and saw Nichelle Nichols, adding her signature to my photograph. We even saw the originals outside of the cons: Takei spoke at the University of South Florida in Tampa on his memories of his time in a Japanese internment camp. William Shatner did a one-man show that came to the Mahaffey Theater in St. Petersburg, FL.

At the Mahaffey, I opted to try something new: a photograph with Mr. Shatner. It was another $80 and I could only stand next to the actor; I could not touch him, though I did say hello. (I was also thrilled that my hand accidentally brushed the tip of his knee when we were preparing for the shot. It was a true accident, but I felt even more special having touched the man). The photographs moved even faster than the autograph session and had with fewer opportunities for conversation, but it was a great shot of the two of us together. I wore my "Go Bold or Go Home" *Star Trek* t-shirt and did the  Vulcan salute next to him. I currently use the image as my faculty photograph and have gotten many comments on it. One person told me that when she first saw the photograph, she thought he was my husband (I wish)!

These days, I go to fewer conventions. They are expensive to attend, parking is difficult, and I do not understand why more of these have not come to my home town of St. Petersburg. The stress to physically arrive at a convention, as, for example, Tampa still undergoes massive construction and hosts many one-way streets, has deterred me from attending all of the cons. Even with pre-purchased tickets, I have found myself contemplating a return home after an hour of gridlock to find parking. Once the car is parked, the conventions, themselves, have new features. Security now stands outside and looks through purses and props. We have to be scanned by a metal detector. The lines exist not only for panel presentations, but also just to get in to the convention. Tickets, even those bought via pre-sale, are picked up only once one stands in another series of lines. Entering the main con is another series of lines. The conventions have become something akin to a day at a theme park:

promises of expensive food and merchandise, crowded conditions, long lines, and herding practices are almost guaranteed.

Somehow, I feel as if the newer conventions lack the heart I associate with my early experiences. They are harder, more brash, and more about being seen than seeing. Selfies abound, as do texted updates. Social media is flooded with moment-by-moment experiences at the convention. The floors have become harder and places to sit are fewer. Fans don't seem to interact with each other quite so much anymore, remaining buried in cell phones or with small cliques. Fandoms are divided up and crowds moved to differing locations. In addition, the convention center is the staple of the convention: it's about the money. What will fans buy? What will they pay? It makes me rather sad at times to see things in such a state.

At present, I am back to attending only Necronomicon. I love the small intimate settings of the homegrown events. I do not know what the future holds for me and conventions beyond my continued participation in Necro. I do find that it gives me an oddly unique bond with some of my students who also go to conventions. I find myself speaking like an old woman when I tell them that in MY day, to become a nerd or a geek one spent time isolated and alone—we earned our stripes by being ostracized. Kids these days have no idea how good they have it with these pre-fabricated convention machines. It is easier, in some ways, to be an individual now than it was then, I think. But, they seem impressed when they hear of my convention experiences of over 30 years. However, I can say that if William Shatner comes to a convention within a two-hour radius of home, I will go, regardless of who puts it together. There is just something about his attitude today—his advice to live life and experience it to the fullest—that I love. His words match my own goals and the center of my soul: embrace life, enjoy it, and experience it. And I shall.

12 WEREPUPS, CONVENTIONS, AND EMOTIONS
Terry Oakes Paine

WerePups

The very first time I took my WerePup™ Jason, to Texas Frightmare Weekend was an adventure. Every few feet we were stopped by someone wanting to see, touch, hold, photograph, or ask a question about him. I was alone that first day and didn't really know anyone but through Jason I instantly fit in and felt like family. The questions ranged from "is he real?" to "did you get him here?" and everything you can imagine in between. We have since added a larger WerePup to our pack, Jemma Rose. (I also have an elf named River Aponi, and a dwarf named Finnick Oliver.)

What is a WerePup, you ask? Well, according to the official WerePups website[3]:

> "WerePups are hyper realistic silicone props, dolls and figures designed and created by creature sculptor Asia Charity Eriksen. They are her original designs representing her own personal take on what a baby werewolf would look like if it were a living

---

[3] If you want more details, you can check out WerePups.com at Hatborohorrorshop.com for information on the artist and her creations.

creature. Their movement appears very fluid and lifelike because of their construction, and when you hold them they have a tendency to move along with your body movements. As you get used to holding and carrying a WerePup, you will learn how to hold them in ways that can fool most people into thinking they saw it move. Most WerePups have solid, platinum silicone head, arms and legs on jointed cloth bodies. The silicone is soft and squishy, but not so excessively squishy that legs and arms are limp - you can bend and squish limbs with ease, but they are firm enough to snap back into place."

The reason I chose a WerePup, initially, is because I love reading books about shifters and I have always preferred canine companions even as a child, when I had a stuffed dog that I carried around. So,  the WerePup was a combination of my two favorite things: babies and canines. Seeing the website for the first time (I don't remember who showed me first) was like finding gold. I had tried vinyl dolls, but they didn't do the trick. Even my elf doll, River, was too inanimate and cold for what I was looking to find. Silicone dolls are expensive and Asia offered a "half down, half before shipping" option that allowed me to make my dream come true.

Jason was created to remind me of my friend, Micheal Edward Mersinger, who had just passed away. He was my best friend for over 25 years. He had red hair and green eyes, just like I requested for Jason. I had called my friend "Jason" because he and I loved watching horror movies together and there were a lot of Mikes around. So that is how Jason Edward came about looking like he does and getting his name.

As far as taking the WerePups to conventions, especially Frightmare, that just sort of seemed natural. I have always had anxiety in crowds and Jason helped take the focus off of me. I had no problem connecting with people through Jason or the others in our pack. Alone, on the other hand, I couldn't speak to anyone or feel the same sense of connection. People remember Jason and me: they would never have remembered me without him.

Conventions

Texas Frightmare Weekend is the brainchild of Loyd Cryer and has been held the first weekend in May, every year since 2006, in Dallas, Texas. Frightmare is a horror convention that is attended by people around the world. Directors, producers, writers, artists, actors, and actresses alike attend, meet, and greet their fans. There are vendor booths for memorabilia, costuming, artwork, and much, much more. It is three days of mingling with people who love the things you love, attending parties, and sharing photo ops. It is so much fun that I haven't missed a year since my first time there! The convention also supports the fundraising efforts of *Stop the Stigma*, a movement to stop the stigma of seeking mental health care.

Ad you might well imagine, since acquiring Jason and Jemma, and taking them with me to Frightmare, celebrity responses to my WerePups have been positive, if not humorous. Meeting Dee Wallace was a trip. When she looked at me quizzically, after seeing the WerePups in the stroller, I told her "well, this is what happens when you mess around in the woods." She responded by telling me "that is just wrong" and laughing; it was too funny. Then every time she saw us come by her booth, I knew she had spotted us, because she would shout out "wrong" and smile when I made eye contact.

Cassandra Peterson, while doing a photo op as Elvira where she held Jason, asked "should I breastfeed?" She is the consummate professional and stays in character when in costume. I loved her all the more for playing along. I went back and got her autograph while she was not in costume, as well, as she wasn't as playful, but still very sweet. I really enjoyed both personas.

Matthew Lillard (who is known for his roles in *13 Ghosts, Scream,* and as Shaggy in *Scooby Doo*), could not handle the WerePups at all

(Jason and Jemma) and made funny faces during our photo op. But he had the photographer take two photos and signed both; no charge for second photo or autograph. I had to send my husband to get the photo autographed, because every time I came near him with the WerePups (not in line to get an autograph, just walking past his table and stopping to watch him interact with others) he would walk the other way, as if afraid. I don't know if they really bothered him or if he was just having fun with us: it seemed a little over the top and performance-like (he had long lines, therefore a huge audience to entertain). I guess we will never know for certain.

I was able to get photos of Jason with Bex Taylor Klaus and Carlson Young, from the TV series *Scream*, for free because they couldn't resist holding Jason when they saw us walk by their table. They were really fun to talk to about the WerePups and I enjoyed watching them take selfies and take turns taking the each other's photo with Jason.

Tony Todd, the Candyman, fell in love with Jemma during our group photo op. He asked us to come by his booth so he could get a better look at her. He had his assistant take photos with his personal phone of us and him with her: I'm guessing to show family and friends. He was so nice and spent a bit of time with us, and gave us a bracelet from his table merchandise.

Billy Zane does not touch anyone when signing autographs. He is a bit of a self-proclaimed germaphobe, but as we approached, he got out his phone and said, "Now this calls for a photo." He took our picture, with Jason, to show his wife and children.

Now when my husband Carl, my friend Christine, and I go to Frightmare, we like to sit in the lobby with our stroller full of WerePups to watch for the stars as they check into the hotel. On one occasion, Meg Foster (most recently from Rob Zombie's *31*) walked over and held Jason, and talked to us for a bit. Later that morning, Claudio Simonetti (music composer from the original *Suspiria*) actually sat on the couch with the three of us and talked and took photos on his phone with the pups. Claudio added Christine as a friend and posted the photos of himself and her pup, Eklund, on his Facebook page.

Eating at the host hotel of Frightmare, the Hyatt Regency DFW, breakfast buffet with a stroller full of pups is fun, too. Not all of the stars who attend conventions utilize room service, so they often stop

to see the pups as they get their breakfast. We also get a lot of attention from staff, stars, and the regular hotel guests alike. It's always fun to make new friends. Everyone can tell the WerePups are there to be seen and so they have no problem coming over to ask questions. The staff from prior years remember us and are excited to see we have returned. They love seeing the costumes we choose for the pack. Costumes include Pirates (Vidor's High School mascot), Things 1-4 (Dr. Seuss) horror movie t-shirts, *Firefly/Serenity* t-shirts, *Nightmare Before Christmas*, Deadpool, and just clothes with their names on them. I try to match, either with wolf contacts in my eyes and "Mom" shirt, or matching shirts/costumes.

We have cards that we hand out to allow those we meet to follow our adventures on Facebook (The Crescent Oak Pack) and also list the Artist, Asia, as well as two websites to help them view more of her artwork and projects.

Emotion

It's not just at conventions that the WerePups are known for attending. Locally, in and around Vidor, Texas, at several Walmart's  and Buc-ee's and at various events where Christine and I sell our crafts, the WerePups have found friends and admirers. In 2018, we stopped in at the Buc-ee's in Madisonville, Texas on the way to Frightmare, took photos, and posted them to Facebook. Everywhere we turned, at Frightmare, people would say "oh yeah, we saw y'all at Buc-ee's!" Sometimes they say that they saw us on Facebook (we always tag Frightmare while traveling there and back home).

Walmart is always an adventure. We get asked all the time if the WerePups are monkeys. We say, "No they are baby werewolves." We get asked if they are real. Even after saying no, we get asked "how old are they?" or "how big do they get?" or "what do you feed them?" It's fun to see all the reactions.

Sometimes people don't show me their reaction openly, which is why my husband likes to hang back and watch how they react after they pass by us. I've gotten it all: fear, shock, humor, and those who think I'm crazy. I often get asked why I carry them. My answers to their questions range from "because I can" to "for emotional support." It all depends on their approach to speaking to me. Sometimes they just laugh at me, so at that point I tell them not to be rude, and state that I wouldn't laugh at their _____ (fill in the blank with whatever they might cherish).

Jason is a registered emotional support animal, and he goes with me everywhere. The rest of my dolls only go out for conventions, or events. The emotional support necessity came about because of my social anxiety and depression. This is caused by, or a side effect of, being on disability since I was 32 years old. I have psoriatic arthritis, fibromyalgia, and several other health issues. Jason, being weighted and feeling like a baby when held, gives that same sense of calm when holding a baby, without being too heavy and causing pain. I have two dogs, but they are 12-15 pounds each and have tiny feet that can sometimes cause more pain and make me feel worse, even when they are trying so hard to comfort. The realistic vinyl babies don't give me the same sense calm: Jason does and has since the first time I held him. At 4.5 lbs. he is worth his weight in gold when I just need to feel calm inside.

I spend a lot of time alone. It can be depressing but looking over and seeing my dolls helps in ways I cannot describe. Unless you have felt isolated and different from everyone you know, this won't make much sense. But I have a letter from my therapist that says having Jason is good and doesn't make me crazy. He is better than any other emotional support animal: he won't die, he doesn't grow up, he doesn't outgrow his clothes, doesn't make a mess or harm anything or anyone—and he doesn't require a veterinarian or anything else that is needed when you have a living emotional support animal.

My husband, friend Christine, our WerePups, and I all recently attended our fifth Texas Frightmare Weekend and we are already looking forward to next year. It was much more crowded than prior years and Jason really helped control the anxiety associated with crowds. We met celebrities and made new friends to add to the ones we look forward to seeing every year. Withdrawal from being around like-minded people and having to re-assimilate into the "real" world again is tempered by connecting with our friends on social media. Established friends and new friends alike are why we love attending conventions. Attending with WerePups just makes it all more special!

Book One: For the Love of the Con

13 A *ROCKY* WEEKEND
Thomas Ward

It is four o'clock, Labor Day morning, and I am terrified.

An exhausted announcer reads my introduction in laconic monosyllables. In a few moments I will be compelled to step onstage and experience what I am certain will be one of the worst moments of my life.

We've been suckered, I think. I stare over my shoulder at my rag-tag gaggle of performers, painted up, costumed, rehearsed to the point of neurosis, and all sure of the same unfortunate truth as I; there was nobody out there. We were about to do our show, the show we had worked so hard for, to a vast empty room.

I've been a slave driver, an asshole. Everyone hates me, and they're right to do so, because it's all been for nothing. I turned back towards the darkened stage. My entrails threaten to exit through my throat as the emcee finishes his banal and largely conjured platitudes about our nascent little alternative theater company.

A single spotlight appears; the emcee says my name, and I take the most reluctant step of my life…

I might be getting ahead of myself. I want to go back a few months…

Book One: For the Love of the Con

We had failed, and we had failed hard. Our fledgling *Rocky Horror* troupe barely hung on through the preceding year. Our original home  in the Conservative suburbs north of Atlanta had proven unfriendly and then untenable. There was rivalry with another cast, a performance cut short when a fight broke out—devolving into a near-riot—and ultimately, our theater went out of business, leaving our cast homeless.

For those unfamiliar, *The Rocky Horror Picture Show* is a 1975 musical send-up of classic horror films and sexual mores starring a young Susan Sarandon, a Bond villain you don't remember, the creepy guy from *Dark City* (not Kiefer Sutherland, the other one) and, a cross-dressing Tim Curry. It has catchy songs, sexual shenanigans, and no plot to speak of. If that sounds ridiculous, that's because it is. This particular piece of inexplicable, post-Dadaist absurdity would have been consigned to B movie history if not for the vagaries of the Keith-Albie model of film distribution and the antics of midnight movie goers in lower Manhattan in the 1970s. At those showings, there was talking back to the movie, singing along to the movie, throwing things at the movie, and even acting out the movie as it played. Fast forward a few decades and you find the modern phenomenon of "shadow-casting," organized performances by volunteer casts that run in tandem with the film, complete with props, costumes, choreography, and audience participation. Even after forty years, such performances are a weekly occurrence in virtually every major city in the Western World. If you've never seen it, you should, especially if you find yourself in Atlanta, and have the chance to see Lips Down on Dixie.

Months without a theater had cost us half of our actors, much of our enthusiasm, and all of our audience. When we did finally find a new, and more centrally located home, we were a shadow of a shadow cast. We worked for six months to rebuild our audience and our talent pool, but it was rough going in a sketchy neighborhood with a sketchy theater owner giving us scant more support than our previous theater uptown. We were beat, and we were close to being beaten.

Then, along came Dragon Con.

Bugsy, our Producer, lobbied for several months to secure us a performance at that annual fan mega-convention. But, the cast leadership had chosen not to broadcast that fact to our members. Such a long shot gig might be just another failure in a long line of disappointments. Dragon Con was firmly ensconced as one of the largest, and certainly the rowdiest, of the convention circuit. We were upstarts, unknowns with no pedigree and no history. Atop that, our rival cast had performed *their* version of *Rocky* at Dragon Con several times in the past and were not amenable to giving it up.

Even now, with sixteen years of hindsight, I do not know how Bugsy did it. Who did he befriend, cajole, or threaten in convincing the Con's leadership to displace our rivals? Suddenly, we had a goal, a destination! We would step onto a strange and fully outfitted stage, not the cement floor of our unadorned movie theater. We would be featured alongside celebrities instead of dodging back alley bums. Most of all, we would perform for an audience of hundreds, not dozens.

Even to someone who has attended a mega-con, indeed, for anyone not into specifically *RHPS* or competitive cosplay, it can be difficult to explain what Dragon Con means. For the fans, it is a chance to pick up rare merch, get autographs with their favorite personalities and authors, and have a rowdy good time. For the bands, it is a gig unlike any other. But, for us, it is the big one; it is the special event, the Broadway, the Super Bowl Halftime. It is the most culturally significant, and the best attended show we perform.

For Dragon Con, our regular Friday night performance would not do. We had to take the show to the next level. We had to blow the doors off. We needed the best show of our collective careers. It wouldn't take much, just two months of constant rehearsal and prop building in a vacant sorority hall in the damp basement of a local student union. We begged favors to upgrade our paltry props, costumes, and set pieces. I wrangled, and agonized, and nit-picked, and berated, and ranted, in the style of directors since the days of the Greek Choruses.

Personalities clashed. The tech team went sleepless. Performers rage-quit and stress-cried. But, we rehearsed the show until we nearly achieved that ephemeral quality that great *Rocky* casts covet, "perfect screen accuracy." We knew all the details: Dr. Scott is left handed. We saw all the quirks: Riff switches hands with the laser gun. We mastered all the challenges: Columbia changes from beaten pajamas into a whale-boned burlesque costume, including a full makeup swap, in 28 seconds. The weekend finally arrived, and we were as ready as we were going to be.

Nothing went right.

From the first moment, the whole weekend went sideways. Dragon Con had recently adopted a new method for issuing participants' badges, creating massive delays and backups. One of the earliest arrivals, I waited in line for five hours. Other cast members waited upwards of eight. This, of course, put everything in our operation behind schedule from the word go.

When the first of us arrived, hours late, the host hotel's manager had concluded that we were not coming, and had removed our table from the performer's concourse to eke out a bit more room in the crowded lanes of traffic. In the years since, Dragon Con has completely revamped the layout for the tables and booths that so many organizations set up at the convention. There are now no booths at all on the concourse that we once occupied and getting around is so much easier than it once was. An hour later, after purloining a table from a neighboring conference room and carrying it overhead through the Con crowd, we were at least marginally functional. We had a table, a tablecloth, a stack of fliers, and a costumed Columbia. However, we still lacked props, giveaway swag, and the items for our silent auction: a cardboard cutout of Tim Curry, and the custom banner we had spent the last pennies in the

Book One: For the Love of the Con

cast treasury to have printed.

All of this was locked in the back of a U-Haul. The crew member charged with bringing those items to us, our Pit Boss, had only just completed his purgatorial stint in the registration line and had hailed a cab to fetch the whole of our casts' possessions. Due to Dragon Con standstill traffic the act of fetching the U-Haul—staged five miles away at our home theater—was a three to four-hour affair. He arrived just in time to pack up for our final dress rehearsal.

Though Dragon Con is famous for being a non-stop event, with official programming sixteen hours a day and unofficial partying overflowing the other eight, we were still committed to a Friday night show at our home theater, one last opportunity to review the minutiae.

Nothing went right.

A careless cast member got lost at the Con, never made it to the theater, and had to be replaced by a less practiced understudy. A leak backstage put several of our performers in damp costumes that ultimately had to be replaced. A drunk patron jumped up on stage and groped our Janet, almost prompting a reboot of the riot that had punctuated our final performance at our original theater. Our Pit

Boss locked the keys in the U-Haul…with the balance of our props and our luggage inside.

A jubilant Saturday and heady Sunday afternoon passed, as we absorbed the convention, taking every opportunity to pimp our show and recruit an audience. A post-dinner run-through in the meeting space allotted as a green room went without incident or error. With smiles all around, we painted and costumed up, tepidly reserving self-congratulation for the curtain call.

Nothing went right.

When we reported backstage at the appointed hour, our props were missing. More specifically, the truck containing our props and set pieces—the same truck that had unceremoniously needed a locksmith the night before—was not at its appointed loading dock. In the era before universal cell phone adoption, our three remaining Pit members set out on foot to locate our wayward roadshow.

In twenty minutes, we had found our Pit Boss, and the truck full of gear that had been systematically denied access to each of the hotel's three loading dock areas. With downtown Atlanta bloated with convention-goers, there was no parking for a mile in any direction. He had been circling the building for almost an hour hoping to find a familiar face he could dispatch to explain the predicament.

He was ultimately allowed to access a dock, but not the one we had been originally promised. We could back up only to a dock for an adjacent ballroom. With our moment less than an hour away, we rushed, in corsets and platform heels, to unload the truck and hand-carry props and set pieces across the hotel concourse through the throngs of intoxicated cosplayers. It is a Saint Curry miracle that we got it all in place so quickly without wrecking something or someone. Though we quickly realized we had no reason to hurry.

Nothing went right.

Our slot was fifth for the night, scheduled to start at 1:00 in the morning. We followed three bands, each with enthusiastic but niche followings that directly circumscribed the geek community, and a headliner that had been a world class act two generations before, but now found themselves invited only because of their freak Hugo award nomination for a seventies-tastic concept album that only hippy uncles and Cultural Studies professors remember. (While the band is known to regular convention attendees, we prefer not to name names due to the unflattering descriptions herein.)

They ran over time. They all ran over time. Band after band ran over. They got chatty with the crowd, played an extra encore, and took too long swapping stage setups. Our appointed hour came and went with two acts still ahead of us. We camped backstage, continuously reapplying makeup and marking out our dance numbers, for hours.

The longer Sunday night wore into Monday morning, the more audience members, exhausted on the final night of a four-and-a-half-day bacchanalia, gave up and returned to their hotel rooms for a last sleep before heading home on Labor Day Monday morning.

The headliner went on at five minutes of before 2:00am, more than an hour after they had been scheduled to finish. The crowd hated them. With a half-dozen albums since they were last on Top 40 radio, they insisted on playing their recent catalog rather than their hits of yesteryear. The late hour dovetailed with the band members' Social Security eligibility, draining the performance of vigor. Twice the lead singer stopped mid-song, threatening to quit the stage in retaliation for ongoing audience walk-outs. Thankfully, they skipped their encore.

Nothing went right.

Every move we planned for that night, every gag, every light position, every dance step, had been ground into muscle memory on the presumption of an empty stage. But, by this time, the road crew was far over their scheduled day, and the band's manager would not authorize the overtime to disassemble the massive and Byzantine drum kit. It would remain onstage, we were told, but we were welcome to throw a sheet over it, or something, if it was in the way.

Of course, it was in the way! A rock star's drum kit the size of a small hatchback in the dead center of the stage is definitely in the way. After two months of nonstop effort, two months of practice on every backwards-travelling dance move and no-glance pivot, and we would be lucky not to fall on ourselves. Not that it would matter. There was no one out there to watch us.

For the fifteen minutes it took the Pit team to stage our gear, we sequestered backstage for some futile final notes and for my best pass at a pep talk. Eyelids drooped, faces sagged, and I made my usual admonishments about the importance of stage presence and my missives about projecting performance to the very back row. And, the emcee started talking.

I step into the light, pupils cinching to pinpricks. Not a whoop, not a holler, from the crowd. I hear my shoes clatter on the stage risers. I stare out into formless black of an empty ballroom.

For weeks I had insisted—browbeaten, into the cast that, if one is to be a performer, one must give up any pretense of pride, or embarrassment; one must relinquish any hesitation at being thought silly. No matter how awkward the moment, no matter your assumptions about who might be watching, you gave it your all. I told them, "If there's just one paying customer, and they sit in the back row, you still owe them the best show you have in you."

Time to take my own medicine.

I belt into the microphone, "I'm a wiiiiiiiiiiiiiiiiiiiiiiiild and an untaaaaaaaaaaaamed thing!"[4] My amplified voice reverbs through the giant space. I can hear the distortion as the reflected sound from the back wall and the vaulted ceiling muddle each other. "I'm a beeeeeeeeeeee with a deadlyyyyyyyyyy sting!"[5]

I stomp on the stage in time to the song, one any *Rocky* veteran knows by heart. A quartet of hands claps along from the darkness. "You get a hit and your mind goes ping! Your heart will pump, and your blood will sing!"[6]

In the final bars, approaching the last lyric, I throw in my best Freddie Mercury, "C'mon'" ... and the wave breaks over me.

The rush of sound shakes the stage, "Rose tint my world keep

---

[4] O'Brien, Richard. Lyrics to "Rose Tint My World." *Rocky Horror Picture Show*, Ode Records, 1975.
[5] O'Brien, Richard. Lyrics to "Rose Tint My World." *Rocky Horror Picture Show*, Ode Records, 1975.
[6] O'Brien, Richard. Lyrics to "Rose Tint My World." *Rocky Horror Picture Show*, Ode Records, 1975.

me safe from my trouble and paaaa-ain!" So many voices, they all muddle together. The last syllable distends with no one sure when to cut off.

The house lights flash, and I look out on a sea of faces, nearly to the back wall, fourteen-hundred people. Fourteen-hundred people had waited out on the concourse, skipping the bands expressly to see us, at five o'clock on a Monday morning.

The show was not perfect, in no small part because of the barely

disguised drum kit. The blocking proved awkward at times. One or two of the gags did not come off exactly as planned. But, the applause was the type that most amateur actors never experience: loud, enthusiastic, sincere, and lengthy. As the sun came up that Labor Day, it was the best (and best attended) show we had ever done.

As we loaded our props, sets, and assorted paraphernalia into that beaten U-Haul, I saw shining grins on exhausted faces. I heard post-ecstatic giggles amid renewed plans for bigger shows, better shows in a now certain future.

I suppose it is a lie to say that nothing went right that weekend. It was Dragon Con, after all. Of course, there was the epic, absurd, excess: the costumes, the decadence, the *otaku* enthusiasm for the marginal and whimsical. For a dozen miscreants that devote each weekend to recreating a Roger Corman-inspired counter-culture sex musical from the disco era, a first Con together feels much like an Oakley Court homecoming.

Looking back, that weekend, that convention, made the decade and a half since then possible. When Dragon Con first tapped us for that show, we were a mayfly troupe of neophytes that had never seen a half-full house. By dawn on that Labor Day, we were a top-level outfit, with the work ethic and the thunderous ovation to prove it. Those months of rehearsal were our adolescence, our age of painful growth and discomfiting discovery. That show, that beautiful, raucous, packed show, was our coming out party, where we showed the world who we were ready to become.

Rose tint my world.

Afterward: The author retired from the Rocky Horror community two years later, but Lips Down on Dixie has evolved into an Atlanta institution. A new

generation of performers continue the classic Midnight RHPS every Friday at Atlanta's historic Plaza Theatre. As of this writing, LDoD has performed annually at Dragon Con for seventeen years. The audience has ballooned to two and a half times that of the 2002 debut. Commensurate with its popularity, LDoD has been moved to the traditional time slot, Saturday at Midnight. The show typically gets underway by one in the morning.

CONVENTIONALLY SPEAKING

Book One: For the Love of the Con

ABOUT THE CONTRIBUTORS AND EDITORS

Kora Addington is a Georgia-native and Dragon Con adventurer with a love for stories; whether they're in good books, anime, or video games. While being a contributor and working on her personal memoir and commentary blog, ConRhetora, she's currently about to begin study for her master's degree in Linguistics, a new and exciting journey after years of studying English and Literature. Some of her favorite stories and experiences in fandom at the moment include John Green's *Turtles All the Way Down, Mob Psycho 100 II,* and *The Legend of Zelda: A Link to the Past.*

Sadie Blackburn is an independent author who lives and writes in Florida, where she is owned by a criminally genius little dog who is currently planning world domination. She is author of *the Phantoms* collection, a series of ghost novels featuring brave female protagonists who face their own fears to right long-ago wrongs. She is also the author of *The Pentecost Chronicles*, an alternate Victorian history adventure series filled with well dressed, rebellious, flamboyant heroes in top hats and steampunk dirigibles. Sadie is a half Native American, half Irish storyteller who was born in Fargo, North Dakota, before being spirited away to Addis Ababa, Ethiopia as an infant, and then to New York, where she was subsequently raised by Germans and Norwegians. Which explains a lot, really.

Marci Bretts is a video and still photographer, editor, and producer, congoer, and organizer. Marci has been attending cons since a teenager and working as a volunteer or staff almost as long. She no longer just "attends" conventions, as she's either working at one or attending on behalf of another con or organization. She brings her work experience in noncommercial television and independent moviemaking to her event work, which includes pop culture cons, social media creation, and Maker events and groups. When not shooting or editing, Marci enjoys whispering to cats.

Leisa A. Clark is an adjunct professor of Humanities and Communication at various colleges. In her spare time, she has been known to work at local theatres and haunted houses. She also creates homemade soaps and chocolate frogs. Leisa is co-editor (with Amanda Firestone and Mary F. Pharr) of *Harry Potter and Convergence Culture: Essays on Fandom and the Expanding Potterverse*; *The Last Midnight: Essays on Apocalyptic Narratives in Millennial Media*; and *Of Bread, Blood and the Hunger Games: Critical Essays on the Suzanne Collins Trilogy*, published by McFarland & Company. She is also the co-author (with Sadie Blackburn and D.V. Zipper) of a crazy 90s-nostalgic space opera called *The Neon Lites: Adventures Beyond Possibility*. Her latest book, *From Welcoming Feasts to Trolley Treats: Reflections on Food in the Potterverse*, was released in fall 2018.

#

Charlayne Elizabeth Denney has a habit of checking people for fangs and living in the dark, and this is how she discovered her own vampires…and Lilly, Marcus, and the rest of the gang living in the *Fangs & Halos* series she writes. When not hanging with vampires, she's the lady who flies around conventions in a wheelchair with a baby werewolf clutched in her arm. Of course, all this stuff weirds out her kids and grandkids. Fond of the darker corners of a good library, she tends to believe the Internet isn't for porn but for doing research. She's been attending conventions in Texas/Oklahoma in one capacity or another since 1979, and found her husband, Bruce, through a want-ad in the program book for ConTroll 93.

Dee Fish is a cartoonist, illustrator, and graphic designer who is the creator of the online comic, "Dandy & Company" (www.dandyandcompany.com), an all-ages humor comic and the semi-autobiographical online comic "Finding Dee" (www.findingdee.com). She is also the writer and artist of the creator owned comic book, "The Wellkeeper" (www.thewellkeeper.com), a young adult fantasy / adventure series. She has also worked on comic stories for "Tellos," "The Perhapanauts," and "The Mice Templar" for Image comics, "Star Mage" and "White Chapel" for IDW Publishing and "Atomic Robo" for Red 5 Comics. She is the co-creator, co-writer, and illustrator for the series "Carpe Noctem" for Hashtag Comics.

Valerie Estelle Frankel is the author of over 60 books on pop culture, including *Star Wars Meets the Eras of Feminism*, *The Many Faces of Katniss Everdeen*, and *How Game of Thrones Will End*. Many of her McFarland books focus on women's roles in fiction, from her heroine's journey guides *From Girl to Goddess* and *Buffy and the Heroine's Journey* to books like *Superheroines and the Epic Journey* and *Women in Doctor Who*. She teaches at Mission College and San Jose City College and speaks often at conventions of all sorts. Come explore her research at www.vefrankel.com.

Sally L. Gage is an anthropologist and Lycanthropologist hailing from Michigan and Florida. Her research and interests focus on the migratory patterns of the North American werewolf. Sally has been featured on the Travel Channel's *Mysteries at the Museum* and has published articles on Sanguinarianism, Lycanthropology, and Vampires. She travels the US with her pack of werewolves and delights young and old with stories of werewolf folklore. Sally is the creator of a series of "Dark journals/blank books" to encourage storytelling in others.

Kathy Lockwood is a university administrator and professor with a background in broadcasting and film. She is also a professional actress and writer, which has allowed her to meet many celebrities and have some entertaining experiences over the years. A sci-fi fan since childhood, she has been attending conventions for over 35 years. Her research interests center around the fan/celebrity relationship, and her first master's thesis, *Participatory Fandom in American Culture*, focused on attendees of Dragon Con. Her first love is writing, and she also holds an MFA in Creative Writing from the University of Tampa. Her book *Twelve Weeks on Tinsmith* details her time working on the film *Edward Scissorhands*.

Joyce McGuire is a full-fledged coffee fiend and Viking at heart with still-limited con experience. She enjoys writing original stories and fanfiction—solo and collaboratively—in her spare time, along with watching a wide array of movies whenever possible. She's a tattoo enthusiast, trying to collect at least a couple more every year. Joyce is also an avid dog lover; she is lucky enough to be mom to two mutts named Mack and Pookie for the last eleven years. She's lived across much of the Eastern Seaboard and American South, always looking forward to the next great adventure in life—especially since recently slaying the dragon called Thyroid Cancer.

Terry Oakes Paine is a daughter, sister, wife, mother, Mimi, and friend—and proud WerePup parent. She loves attending Texas Frightmare Weekend with her WerePups, husband, and friend. She collects Pop figures, fairies, and *Friday the 13th* memorabilia. This is her first time writing for publication. She lives in Vidor, Texas with her husband, Carl. Her children are grown, and make her proud every day. Her grandchildren light her world.

Mara H. Sansolo is a software trainer and consultant by day, and Backstreet Boys fangirl the rest of the time. Academically speaking, she holds Graduate and Post-Graduate degrees in Library Science, Instructional Design, and E-Learning. And speaking of BSB, she has been on five cruises with them, including the European one. There is no limit when it comes to Mara and the Backstreet Boys (in fact, she two BSB tattoos). When not fangirling, Mara enjoys spending time with her four-legged baby, Gretchen, who is the love of her life. She currently resides in Lakeland, Florida.

Brandy Stark is a Florida resident and a lifelong science fiction fan. She grew up on cartoons, comic books, and *Star Trek* which currently manifests in her Humanities teachings for various institutions of higher education. When existing in the space/time of Earth Prime, Dr. Stark creates hand-wrapped wire metal sculptures depicting creatures of fantasy. These have shown and won awards in numerous conventions, including San Diego Comic-Con, World Fantasy Con, and Dragon Con. She is also an aficionado of the paranormal world and has spent 22 years investigating local haunted locations, ghost lore, and urban legends. She founded the SPIRITS of St. Petersburg in 1997 and has spoken on ghostly lore for numerous organizations. She is the host of the Paranormal Pets podcast found on Petliferadio.com.

Thomas Ward, beginning with VulKon in the early 90's, is a veteran of over fifty Cons, from Comic to Momo to Frolic to Dragon. He is a skydiver, cigar smoker, and avid collector of vintage *Star Trek* action figures. Professionally, he is a Production Coordinator for film and television, contributing to such properties as *Ant Man & the Wasp, Ozark,* and *Pitch Perfect 3*. Thomas and his wife, Dr. JoDi Lynn Osborn, reside in Decatur, Georgia with their dog, Smidgen. He very much recommends you see LDoD perform at Atlanta's historic Plaza Theater.

COMING SOON FROM MHP PUBLICATIONS

CONVENTIONALLY SPEAKING II: ELECTRIC BUGALOO

(Creators, Makers, Authors, and Artists share their convention experiences)

&

CONVENTIONALLY SPEAKING III: WE'LL HAVE A GAY OLD TIME

(The LGBTQ+ con-going experience)

Made in the USA
Columbia, SC
06 July 2019